# Summer of '74

## A Comedy in Three Acts

by
Liam Scheff
&
S.C.V. Taylor

Copyright © 2013 Liam Scheff & S.C.V. Taylor
Cover and comic art by Liam Scheff. All rights reserved. Do not reproduce in any media format without express written permission from the authors, but please do enjoy and share the book itself, or recommend it to friends - with our thanks.

ISBN-13: 978-1482591453
ISBN-10: 1482591456

PRODUCTION NOTES

"Keep it loose."

Words matter; they drive scenes to action goals, they connote as much as they describe. Their strategic positioning, careful deployment, and even their intentional absence can raise a scene to heights, or sink it to flagging despair. But dogmatic literalism is the death of creativity. Simply put: keep it loose. This play is intended to be above all things, fun – for the audience and the performers. Keeping that in mind, the style should be 'light improvisation.' Players must respect the structure and purpose of each scene but they'll find ample room to stretch and experiment within the form. We believe that a play released to the public and performers will gain through the interpretation of parts by gifted actors and directors. To wit: if you find something that works well or is particularly hilarious, please let us know.

- The Playwrights, February 2013

# Table of Contents

Scenes and Set Decoration — vi

Cast of Characters — viii

Act 1 — 1

Act 2 — 19

Act 3 — 39

About the Authors — 63

S74 Comic Preview — 65

## SCENES AND SET DECORATION

DESERT – California desert. Pale, flat, hot with scrub brush and mountains in the distance.

MAIN STREET, BARSTOW – One and two-story buildings line the small town center; the shops on Main Street are mom and pop businesses that have seen better days. The whole town looks like an idyllic hamlet from the 1950s after a 25-year decline.

DAY-GLO BAR & GRILL - The "Day-go bar." A large bar and grill on Main St. near the beauty salon, resembling the bar in Edward Hopper's Nighthawks: large windows peering in at late night drinkers and a central island soda-fountain bar with its interior strangely visible from the street. UNCLE BEN is co-owner with a silent partner (Mr. Jabah). The "L" in the sign "Glo" is burnt out, giving the impression of "Day-Go-Bar".

BARSTOW BEAUTIES - The beauty salon on Main St. where Candy, Princess and Aimiee to gossip and prettify.

BOBA'S CURRY PALACE - At the far end of Main street, at the edge of the commercial district, a large two-story building, converted from a failed Hare Kirhna temple. It manages to keep its doors open due to repeat business by loyal customers who usually referred to as "chinese food".

DR. VADER'S HOUSE - A modern California take on Frank Lloyd Wright - a large one-story ranch house with too many windows and mirrors, an open round pool/patio in the back with torchlight; home to Doctor Vader's private office, and, by a short stone path, to his private practice.

LUKE AND AIMIEE WALKER'S HOUSE - A slightly dumpy but well-maintained cottage house a couple miles outside of downtown. It's got an unusually large extra bedroom which serves horticultural purposes.

DJIOUWASKI'S JUNKYARD – Typical junkyard, except this one has a small house in front. It's a shack of a building but cozy.

NANA'S HOUSE - Right downtown, a block off of Main St. in the would-be 'chic' block or two of Barstow. A private, decorated apartment in the town's only upscale apartment building, decorated a bit like a Fabergé egg.

MO'S ISLAND TRUCK STOP - An oasis in a sea of dust. A transportation hub where every species of human intermingle and refuel: 50s greasers in classic cars, bikers, hippies in VW bus, Marines in a jeep, families in campers, Elvis impersonators, prostitutes, townies, senior tourists on a bus. Gas is 55 cents/gal.

COUNTY FAIR – The Barstow county fair is a picture-book American rural traveling carnival with rides, games, food stands, tents, a classic car show, and the featured event -- the Nakamuri Traveling Samurai Exhibit. We should see lots of lights, balloons and exciting amusements.

**VEHICLES:**

There are three 'starring' vehicles, plus any that you'd like to create for traffic. The vehicles are constructed in a forced 3/4 perspective, so that the side is entirely visible along with the front window of the vehicle, facing the audience.

HAN'S VAN - Han's roaming home. The classic 70s van is built with a false 3/4 view so that the entire front seat is visible, as though at an angle - with an extended front seat window so that the rumble seat behind the two front seats is also visible from the side. The passenger side should be built as a hinged drop-down (or removable) panel to reveal the interior. A shag carpet and bed, with a disco ball hanging, and a large 8-track and tape player, music posters, decorate the inside. The Van also has to have a changeable side panel to represent its first emblem (reclining fantasy female figure), its in-progress painting of the falcon, and the final, finished falcon. The middle should be covered by large brush-strokes. The final should look reasonably good, but not professional.

TIGH'S POLICE INTERCEPTOR – a modified muscle car that Tigh 'traded' Mr. Jabah's kid for letting him out of a large drug bust. It has a comically large hemi protruding from the hood and is built in the same ¾ view style as the van.

AIMIEE'S LONG-FINNED CADILLAC with a TRAILER – A late 60s model convertible Cadillac that's well maintained, but not too pretty. Built in ¾ view, it also has a small "U-Haul" type trail attached to the back. The trailer is labeled as a "4TOW-2U" trailer, and has a handle on the back bumper.

## CAST OF CHARACTERS

HANSEL DJIOUWASKI (pronounced "ja-waw-ski") - 24, a roguish, straight-shooter with simple Midwestern good looks. He runs a package delivery service and drives a sweet custom van which comes to be known as the "Bicentennial Falcon." A bit of Luke Wilson.

PRINCESS LEAH VADER - 17, a self-possessed, Jewish, beautiful brunette. She is currently dating Hansel, but she knows she can do better. She is counting the days until she leaves Barstow to go off to College back east. A bit of Anne Hathaway, Lindsay Lohan, a young Laura Flynn Boyle.

CHEWEY COYOTL - mid 20s, tall, Native American/Aztec. He wears a leather cap, old motorcycle goggles with a long vertical black rubber nose guard (resembling a dog's nose - to protect it from getting broken again), a large scruffy but straggly beard, and leather coat with fringe on the sleeves, cuffs and edges. He only speaks in MOANS because he's always high; only Han understands him.

LUCAS "LUKE" WALKER - 16, a sweet, earnest kid, frustrated with his life in this small desert town, but loves martial arts and Bruce Lee. A bit of Richie Cunningham, a bit of young Mark Hamill.

DR. DON VADER - 42, a doctor of gynecology and proctology and head of the Republican Party in Barstow. He's a swinger who hosts key parties and ogles women without shame and has a special relationship with President Nixon. A laWill Farrell.

AIMIEE WALKER - 40, Luke's mother, an aging Vegas showgirl, sex-bomb stripper and pistol toting smoker with a mind for business. A la Elizabeth Shue.

BEN WALKER - 50, an embittered gay alcoholic who owns a bar in town and is always telling stories whether anyone is listening or not. He is Aimiee's cousin and Luke calls him "Uncle Ben." Entirely Paul Lynde.

CANDY VADER - 38, Don Vader's neglected wife. She comes from money and defied her father to marry the young doctor. Now she regrets it, but is a traditionalist and unable to divorce.

NANA YIOTTA VADER - 70, German/Hungarian, walks with a cane but is spry for her age. Used to be a flapper and lived the high life in Berlin, dancing for the Nazis. Isn't sure who Don Vader's father was. Jewish, but not religious. A confidant for Princess. A bit of Dr. Ruth.

CHARLES CULSHAW CARRINGTON III, aka "C3", 20s, is a smooth-talking psychedelic 70s disco king from London of African decent. He wears gold-lamé, has a huge afro, gold cape, shorts, sunglasses and roller-skates.

SHERIFF TIGH - 30s, small-town, small-minded country Sheriff who looks the other way for special favors. He considers Han his nemesis and is always plotting ways to "catch him in the act." A touch, but not too much, Roscoe P. Coltrane; a bit of Sheriff (Smokey and the Bandit)

AUNT ELISE DJIOUWASKI - 50s, Hansel's aunt. Old world Catholic, speaks very little English. Loves Hansel dearly.

UNCLE DJIOUWASKI - 50s, Hansel's uncle. Old world Polish Catholic who escaped the Nazis and Stalin and came to America. He is devout and superstitious, and doesn't like Princess.

SENSEI MIKE - 30, long blonde hair and a bushy mustache, a PTSD-scarred Vietnam Veteran, he is very intense and is Luke's mentor.

ANTHONY "GUIDO" SANCHEZ - 28, fat, bright but streetwise, from Mexico city, with a few big pimples and greasy hair. He works for Mr. Jabah. He wears t-shirts a size too small, and is a huge movie buff.

MR. JABAH *(pr. Ja-báh)* "JABAH THE JEW" - Never-seen but often referred to. Late 30s, a local kingpin who controls most of the illegal activity from San Bernadino to Vegas. He is the co-owner of Mo's Island and the Day-Glo Diner, and uses both as fronts for his other business activities. He is a Russian Jew, a former star of the Moscow Circus. While touring outside of Russia, he defected and came to America. He always talks about how wonderful American is because its the land of (criminal) opportunity.

MAUREEN "MO" ISLEY - Co-owner of Mo's Island - ex-wife of a founding member of the Isley Brothers (musical group), a long-time waitress, in the "Flo" mold from Alice. A tough woman of business, she's cheeky, worldly, and madam of the truck stop prostitutes. She can be quite friendly in her way. A bit of "Flo" from the "Alice" TV series.

DJANGO PHETT - 40s, Sri Lankan, owner of "Boba Phett's Curry Palace" the only "Oriental" restaurant in town. He is a soft-spoken but warm man and has a soft spot for Hansel, one of his best customers.

BOBA PHETT - 40s, Django's wife, from India.

PRIYA PHETT - 16 going on 17, smart, sweet, respectful and loving to her parents. She likes Hansel but is waiting for him to figure out that he's in a rut, and needs to pull himself out.

## MINOR & BIT CHARACTERS
*(Can be played by supporting players using costumes and wigs for individual looks)*

SEXY REDHEAD - Women in her early-mid 20s, very good-looking, beautiful long hair, med-low cut top, and a chic stylish miniskirt.
GEORGE - A mysterious man with a short, groomed beard wearing a flannel shirt and jeans. He is watching everything with deep interest and seems to be taking notes.
LIBRARIAN - 40, very pleasant-looking woman with her hair in a bun, and reading glasses.
AZTEC STONER - dresses like Chewey and sounds like Cheech Marin. Much easier to understand than Chewey.
PARTY GIRL #1 - key party guest.
PARTY GIRL #2 - key party guest.
WARREN - key party guest, Warren Beatty look-a-like.
CARLY - key party guest, Carly Simon look-a-like.
NAOMI - 30s, long legs, big boobs, not that bright, but strong enough to put Don in his place.
CARNIVAL BARKER

# ACT ONE

## SCENE 1

OUTER SPACE DISCO

*In front of the curtain, or without lighting the full stage (only the lip). A low FOG covers the stage as the curtain rises on a dark backdrop. A DISCO BALL spins showering the stage with tiny dancing points of light or stars. We are in OUTER SPACE.*
*MUSIC PLAYS. "Night on Disco Mountain" by David Shire.*
*A tall, dark mysterious figure in gold lamé on roller skates dances out onto the stage. The skater, "C3" skate-dances across the stage as we hear space battle sounds – the roar of a TIE FIGHTER, the PEW PEW of a laser blast.*
*As the fog clears and the dancing man skates off, the lights change and we find ourselves on Terra Firma, in the Desert.*

## SCENE 2

CALIFORNIA DESERT - OUTSIDE BARSTOW - 1974

*A 1970s custom American-make van with a teardrop window in the rear. The van is a built and painted as a cheated 3/4 view so all of the front and drivers side is visible. A long side window reveals a 'back seat' so that three characters are clearly visible in the van. A 1973 Interceptor sports car converted into a roaring police car, with a hemi jutting out of the hood, is in pursuit with LIGHTS and a WAILING SIREN. The car set pieces face the audience side by side and rock back and forth simulating forward movement. The vehicles will always travel stage left to stage right except as noted.*
*The driver of the van is HANSEL DJIOUWASKI ("Jawaski"), a roguish, ruggedly appealing straight-shooter. His co-pilot is CHEWEY, 20s, a tall, Native American/Aztec who wears a leather cap with ear flaps, old motorcycle goggles with a long vertical black rubber nose*

guard. Chewey only speaks in moans and grunts because he's so high all the time - but Han seems to understand him.

HAN. It's now or never, Chewey! *(Chewey flips a switch on the dash that glows green. Han and Chewey wait for it and -- NOTHING. Han hits the dash exasperated. Chewey MOANS.)* Come on, girl. Come on!
SHERIFF TIGH. I've got you now!

*(ACTION SCENE: The sounds of ENGINE ROARS accompany a jockeying of the car and van cut-outs. Tigh's Interceptor pulls ahead and blocks the van. Han slams on the brakes and hits the wheel in frustration. We hear a long SCREEECH and SKID OUT. Some fog or smoke on stage. SCREECHING TIRES, then silence. Tigh swaggers out of his car over the van's driver.)*

TIGH. Well, well, well...Smuggling again, Jewiski, you cocky, S.O.B., I got you this time. Looks like yer jig is up, Han-sel!
HAN. *(smooth, leaning out the window)* It's HAN!
CHEWEY. *(grunts defiantly)* ARRRUGH.
TIGH. Alright Jewiski, let's have that truck open, smuggler!
HAN. I ain't smuggling' nothing. And besides, everybody knows you got that car from Jabah's kid for lookin' the other way.
CHEWEY. *(in agreement).* Rurrgghh.
HAN. You said it, Chewey. Who's the smuggler now?
TIGH. Why you cotton-picking son of a Pollack Jew immigrant bastard!
HAN. It's Djiouwaski *("Ja-waw-ski")*. I ain't Jewish, you moron. And second of all--
TIGH. I ain't got no car illegal-like! I'm gonna run you in this time, boy!

*(The fight is cut short when the back door swings open and out slides-- A WHITE OVER THE KNEE LEATHER BOOT.*
*PRINCESS, 17, self-possessed, Jewish, brunette, beautiful, in a white mini-skirt and thin white summer top, no bra, steps out and struts up to Tigh, flirting, confident,*

*sexy. Tigh is under her spell.)*

PRINCESS. Hiiii, Tiiiigh.
TIGH. Oh, um, uh. I mean, hello hi, Princess. I didn't know you was in there!
PRINCESS. Were we speeding? I'm sorry. Han was just giving me a ride home -- and you know how Daddy doesn't like to be kept waiting *(wrinkling her nose).*
TIGH. Oh, yeah, I sure know that, Princess. I surely do. Well what are you standing around here for? Best you get home to your Father. Make sure to tell him I says "Hi."
PRINCESS. I sure will...

*(Han shoots Tigh a smirk. Tigh looks at Han and squints, promising a rematch. Han pulls the van onto the road with a VROOOM of the engine.)*

PRINCESS. *(thinking out loud)* I hate doing that. It makes me feel...dirty.*(Chewey MOANS his appreciation, but Han is clueless. She now addresses Han.)* I wouldn't have to do that if you'd drive at something resembling the speed limit.
HAN *(pauses, glances back then back at the road, waiting for a rejoinder to come to him).* Thanks Mom, I'll drive however I want.
*(The argument continues as the scene changes. "Oh yeah - well," and "I'm sorry it's such a hardship for you, Princess!" etc - improvise as the van drives into - )*

## SCENE 3

DOWNTOWN BARSTOW

*Barstow 1974 has a small main street with mom and pop shops including: Barstow Beauties (salon), the Tae Kwon Do Studio, the Day-Go Bar and others. It is the unimpressive "wanna be" downtown of a rural region - and everyone clearly knows - and is a little tired of - everyone else.*
*Scenes 3, 3-A, 3-B and 3-C take place consecutively on the Main Street set.*

*Several people walk down Main Street including an old woman - about 70, hunched over and walking with a cane - but we get the feeling she's more spry then she looks. This is Nana Yiotta, Princess's grandmother.*

PRINCESS. *(losing patience, exhales in exasperation)* You know, you could say "thank you."
HAN. I'll thank you later *(turning to Chewy and winking).*
PRINCESS. Oh, you mean sex? That's very clever. I wish you were half as clever in bed.
HAN. Whadya mean?
PRINCESS *(Leans out the window and waves).* Hi Nana! *(back to Hansel)* Like...uhm...doing that "something special" for me.
NANA. *(Brightens seeing Princess. Her accent is German)* Hallo Meine Leibchen! Vill I see you later?
PRINCESS *(to Nana).* Yes, after the salon!
HAN. Somethin'? *(pauses to think)* Oh, you're reading that Cosmo again. Look...Nobody does that in real life. It ain't sanitary.
PRINCESS. *(back to Hansel).* You know, you are really such a stu--

*(HORN BLARES. Han hit the horn as DJANGO PHETT, 44, owner of the Indian restaurant, crosses, waving apologetically as he carries 40 pounds of potatoes and carrots in bags on his shoulder and dangling by his side)*

DJANGO PHETT. Sorry! Very sorry! Good day! Good day! Very sorry! *(The van pauses, and then starts again across the stage.)*
PRINCESS. *(out the window)* See you later, Nana! Love you! *(Nana waves.)*
HAN. You're not sore, are ya?
PRINCESS. Let me out.
HAN. But we're going to Boba's for lunch.
PRINCESS. Let me out. *(She continues with increasing volume, as Han is driving, looking out the window, but not hearing her.)*
Let me Out.
Let. Me. Out.

*(Then, one final loud shout)*
LET ME OUT of this piece of SHIT van, you hillbilly MORON! *(The VAN lurches to a halt. Everyone bounces slightly forward. The back door opens with a 'clack' and Princess jumps out; she slams the back door as hard as she can.)*
HAN. *(leaning confidently out the open window, matter-of-factly)* So, I guess I'll be picking you up later...as usual.
PRINCESS. *(storms to the beauty salon)* Whatever.
HAN. *(as the van pulls away)* Can you believe that Chewey? "Somethin' special." What, does she thinks I'm a queer? *(thinking aloud)* Cosmo...
FEMALE VOICES. *(as Princess walks into the SALON).* Hi Princess!

SCENE 3-A

*The van drives away. We see DJANGO PHETT on the sidewalk, who is now joined by his 16-year-old daughter PRIYA, who is helping with the bags.*

DJANGO. Daughter, I should be sorry we've brought you to this town where you can find no proper husband. No one from home! From India!
PRIYA. Or Sri Lanka.
DJANGO. Yes, yes, like your silly father, but your mother would prefer an Indian boy...or, perhaps, she only wants you to be happy.
PRIYA. You worry too much, father. This is my home, after all. Krishna will provide me a husband, I have faith. *(A few potatoes fall from the bag).* Oh, you're losing potatoes! *(They pick up a the potatoes and secure the bag.)*
DJANGO. You're a good daughter, Priya, I hope you are right. I'd feel ashamed if we brought you here only to run a restaurant all your life.
PRIYA *(almost offstage).* But, father, I like the restaurant!

## SCENE 3-B

TAE KWAN DO STUDIO

*Through the glass we see LUCAS "LUKE" WALKER. He is doing his Kata very, very seriously. SENSEI MIKE has long blonde-brown hair and a mustache. He's strong and in his mid-late 20s. He is a very intense PTSD-scarred Vietnam Veteran. Mike is leading him around the room, holding up his hands like pads, letting Luke attack, block, attack, block.*

SENSEI MIKE. That's it Luke! They could be anywhere! *(Luke kicks, turns, punches, turns, blocks - doing "Kata")* Good, Luke! Never judge an opponent by their size - remember the Cong, Luke! Remember the Cong!
LUKE. Cha! Cha! Cha! Ki-YA!

*(Both reciting their Kiya's. Luke is, as always, earnest, sincere and devoted in his martial arts - and not bad, for being a bit small. The lesson finishes. Luke bows to Sensei Mike, who bows back.)*

LUKE. Thanks, Sensei Mike! See you Thursday!

*(He finishes his lesson, bows to his sensei, puts on his white backpack, holds his thumbs in the straps and walks out to Main Street. He stops to look into a storefront window, mindlessly.)*

## SCENE 3-C

INSIDE THE HAIR SALON ("BARSTOW BEAUTIES.")

*Three Women are inside, sitting in chairs facing the audience and Main Street. They talk as they are having their hair done. Princess, her mother, Candy and Lucas' mom, Aimiee. Candy Vader is an East Coast woman of money who married the wrong man and lives a miserable kept existence. She copes through alcohol and denial. Aimiee Walker, 40s, is an aging Vegas showgirl, sex-bomb stripper who has a mind for business but is still a caring mother. On Main Street, Luke walks by. Princess waves at him from behind the beauty salon window.

PRINCESS. Hiiii, Lukey!
LUKE *(already looking at her, waves back enthusiastically).* Hi Princess!
CANDY VADER. Princess... you're not, um, "spending time" with that boy, are you?
PRINCESS. What? Oh, Mom, you're such a perv. *(Candy bristles, and looks at Aimiee for confirmation. Aimiee is looking for polite words of discouragement; Princess looks at both of them, and interrupts as Aimiee is about to speak.)* Oh, relax! It's not like that. He's just a sweetie.

*(Outside the Hair Salon, Luke continues on down the sidewalk and passes, DR. DON VADER, 40, tall, fairly handsome, overly confident, self-proclaimed King of Barstow. He's wearing white slacks and a light blue thin v-neck sweater; a Don Juan in his own mind. Vader sees Luke and smiles. Luke waves in an uncomfortable greeting.*
*Vader continues down the sidewalk and passes in front of the three ladies in the salon, but doesn't see them - he's looking at an approaching woman. The girls are watching him through the 'window.' A luscious mid-20s young woman, perhaps an office worker or secretary on a lunch-break walks by, buxom and quite self-consciously sexy, in a low-cut blouse and high skirt. Vader stops and watches her pass. Vader's remarks follow her as she passes him, and walks on.)*

DR. VADER. Well, Helllleeeeeewwwww... Hello Mrs. Right. And I mean, "right now!" *(Vader bends over at the waist to peer at her legs)* Let's see what's shaking downtown! Ooh. I love the southern view!

*(The woman walks and does not stop; she seems to concentrate more and more on ignoring him as she walks on - tilting her nose - is she slightly flattered? But totally grossed out? Inside the salon, Princess is mortified. Candy pretends it didn't happen. Aimiee chokes back a guffaw. They're all disgusted.*

*Vader, his head at knee level, has wrapped himself into a pretzel - he is now looking backward at the beauty salon window - and at the three women. He realizes where he is and who is watching him and pops up to full attention, facing them.)*

DR. VADER. *(vamping, trying to get himself out of there)* UHHHMMM.... I... Left the... stove on... the cat was... playing... the piano. I think hear my alarm! Is that an air raid? *(Runs off-stage with an exaggerated 'clod, clod, clod!', his platform shoes thudding on the stage.)*

AIMIEE. That guy is such...
CANDY. I can't believe I'm married to that...
PRINCESS. Dad is such a total...
PRINCESS/AIMIEE/CANDY. Asshole! *(Candy takes a sip of her cocktail – she drinks at the salon – trying to shut him out.)*
PRINCESS. I'm so glad I'm getting out of this town.
CANDY. I don't know what I'll do here without you, Princess. With just your father...alone.
AIMIEE. Where are you going to college, Princess?
PRINCESS. Far, far away from here. Well, really Swarthmore. Or Radcliffe, or Wellesley. I got into all of them.
CANDY. Just me and your father, all alone. Oh, maybe dad was right about him.
PRINCESS. Mom... you should really divorce him, you know.
CANDY. Princess!
PRINCESS. It's 1974! Not the dark ages.
CANDY. We don't divorce in our family, dear. My father wouldn't allow it.
PRINCESS. Mom, you can just sue grandpa for the money. He can't hold that over your head.
CANDY. Dear God, Princess. How do you know these things? Oh, I need a drink.
PRINCESS. Or a joint! Come on, mom, it'll help you relax.
AIMIEE. Oh, that reminds me! I gotta go, girls! Time to pay the meter! *(Aimiee leaves in a slight hurry)* Bye, girls! *(They give a "Bye, Aimiee!" We see Luke walking further down the street, where, across one intersection is the--)*

## SCENE 3-D

DAY-GO-BAR

*"Day-Glo," but the "L" is burnt out in the neon sign. Backdrop and scenery. Reminiscent of Edward Hopper's "Nighthawks" Diner. Sitting at the bar is the solitary figure of Ben Walker, 50, an embittered gay alcoholic who is always telling stories whether anyone listens or not. In the mold of Paul Lynde. Luke walks past, then stops.*

LUKE. (*aside*) Oh, I should say hi to uncle Ben...

*(Luke enters the diner and sits next to Ben. A few seats over by the wall sits GEORGE, 30, a curious man with a short, groomed beard, big glasses, a flannel shirt and jeans. He seems to be watching everything with deep interest.)*

BEN. Oh, Hey Luke. It's good to see you. Whadya doing? That karate stuff you do? I did some of that I the war. Did I tell you I was in the war?
LUKE. Wel-
BEN. Here, have a seat, young Luke, you and I should have a chat. You're about all grown up, now, aren't ya?
LUKE. Uh -
*(Ben launches into a soliloquy, pausing only to drink and smoke. Luke tries to speak, but Ben doesn't let up.)*
BEN. So, is your mom still growing those, uh, plants? She still working in Vegas? They make a pretty penny over there...This place would bury me alive if I didn't have a silent partner. *(loud hoarse whisper)* Pssst - It's that Jabah's kid. So, you're still wondering' who your dad is, huh? Let me tell you a secret, young Lucas. And I mean, you could throw a stone and hit, say...any doctor's house within a mile. *Within a mile.* (*a beat, then*) Did you know I knew your mother before she got into the business? Yeap.
LUKE. Uh -
BEN. Vegas was a God-send for her. Through the whole 'father' thing, too. She was a mess, poor thing. Just a young girl, with that asshole...Vegas! That Robert Goulet - now

there's a nice looking man. Sam wa!
LUKE. We -
BEN. Did you know your fa...Doctor...Vader...we were in the war together? Over there in Korea. "The Big K." Oh, man. Oh, MANDY! The stories I could tell. The stories...
LUKE *(gets up and pulls his backpack on).* Okay Uncle Ben. I gotta run! *(exits and waves to Ben)* Boy, old Ben and his crazy stories!
*(Alone on his perch, Ben orders another round as Luke walks offstage. LIGHTS DOWN.)*

SCENE 4

STAGE RIGHT - MAIN STREET (AN HOUR LATER)

*Han is parked in an empty lot on the edge of Main St. He has a cart with paining supplies and a few beer bottles. Han is painting a new emblem on the van. He's painting over the existing emblem - a reclining, supine female, kneeling back, facing an American flag that seems to be bathing her. He's covering her image and painting a large black/blue bird. Princess walks by with a couple bags from the boutique on her arm - she's been shopping.*

PRINCESS. What's that?
HAN. What?
PRINCESS. What is that thing you're painting?
HAN. *(proudly)* It's the bicentennial eagle. We're gonna win the best mural at the county fair.
PRINCESS. *(pauses to consider, then)* Han. It's 1974. The bicentennial is in 2 years.
HAN. I'm getting it done in advance - If I wait til '76, then everybody will have one. *(Princess rolls her eyes, shakes her head.)* Looks pretty good, don't it?
PRINCESS *(looks closely for a moment, then laughs).* That's a falcon, you moron.
HAN *(looks at the mural, then at a little picture taped to the van, which he's painting from).* A what?
PRINCESS. A falcon, your dork.
HAN. Hey, who you callin' a dork?
PRINCESS. Uhg...*(she groans in disgust).*

*(Han looks intently at the picture, a music and light cue send us to --*

### SCENE 4-A

CENTER STAGE - LIBRARY (FLASHBACK)

*Days earlier, Han is in the town library. The library set has one or two tall bookshelves with reference books - big dictionaries and encyclopedias - and a counter toward the back, behind which is the LIBRARIAN. Han stands to the side of one shelf, out of view of the librarian. He runs his finger across the bindings of the Encyclopedia Britannica and grabs the "C-D-F" volume. He holds it open at his ribcage, and flips the pages back and forth quickly.*

HAN. Daffodil, Elephant...Eagle.

*(Han smiles, then begins to rip the page, but the LIBRARIAN. 40, very pleasant-looking woman with her hair in a bun, and reading glasses, walks past and Han, throws the book closed and pretends to be looking for something else. The librarian sees him and Han returns a charming-though-devilish smile. She returns to her desk, and he flips through the book - but his attention is spent peering around the bookshelf at her to see if she's watching him. He glances down only quickly, grabs a page and while pretending to sneeze/cough to cover the sound of paper ripping, he tears a corner of the page out of the book.*
   *Suspicious, the librarian follows Han and is about to catch him, but she crashes into a cart of books, sending them to the floor. When she regains her composure, Han is gone. She looks on the shelf and finds the encyclopedia volume, opens it and holds up the messily torn page. She then reads aloud, turning the pages back and forth.)*

LIBRARIAN. "Factory... Falkirk?" *(She shakes her head as if disappointed with all of humanity.)*

11

STAGE RIGHT - BACK TO PRESENT

    PRINCESS. *(following the Librarian's line)*. Falcon!! *(laughing)* It's a falcon...
    HAN. *(looks at the torn encyclopedia page taped to the side of the van, reading)*. "Fal..."
    CHEWEY. *(amused)*. Rurrugggghhruuh!!
    HAN. Laugh it up, fuzzy! *(to Princess)* Hey, it's fine like it is. Not everyone's a college snob.
    PRINCESS. Technically, I'm only a high school graduate.
    HAN. Shut up.

(LIGHTS DOWN)


## SCENE 5

BARSTOW - DUSTY NEIGHBORHOOD

    *End of the day. The background changes, and we now see a RED-GOLDEN SUN lower in the sky along a long semi-rural road, with houses increasingly spaced. Luke is walking home after leaving the Day-Glo Diner. Luke comes in from stage right continuing his walk home.*
    *STAGE LEFT - reveal a parked car - Tigh's Interceptor. There seems to be a woman in the front seat, but only her mane of feathered hair is occasionally visible, bobbing a bit. She is evidently 'servicing' the Sheriff, out of sight of the audience and Luke.*
    *Luke, far STAGE RIGHT, can't make out what's happening. He is looking around, taking in the pleasant evening. As he approaches the car, he slowly, shamefully realizes what is going on - and who the woman is.*

    TIGH. Oh yeeeaaahhh. Oh, yeah. *(Tigh notices Luke)* Oh, no. *(and realizes who he is)* OH, NO!!
    AIMIEE *(disturbed by the noise, pops her head up out of Tigh's lap, wipes her mouth, and leans her head out of the window, she is non-plussed)*. Oh, hey, Luke honey!
    TIGH. Oh, GOD NO!
    AIMIEE. Luke, sweetie! I left some chinese food from Boba's on the counter! I'll be home soon. Don't forget to

water the plants! *(Luke silently shudders and walks purposely, stiffly away from what he's just seen - clearly not for the first time. He's entirely clenched.)*
AIMIEE *(to Tigh)*. He's such a good boy.
TIGH. Oh God.

### SCENE 6

### STAGE LEFT - JUNKYARD / HANSEL'S HOUSE

*This will be a parallel scene with two scenes playing back and forth (intercutting) between actors and sets STAGE LEFT - Hansel's home in the junkyard and - STAGE RIGHT - Princess at Nana's house in a nice suburban part of town.*

*The two houses are a study in contrasts, poor and wealthy, and world views - (Jawaski's) pessimist and (Nana's) rather opportunistic optimist (she makes her own fate).*

*The Jawaski's: it's a shack of a building on a lot on a outskirts of town. Han's van is parked outside. HANSEL, AUNT ELISE and UNCLE are sitting to eat their traditional Polish dinner - purple cabbage, potatoes, carrots and bread. Uncle is a short man and easily excited, very old world and a superstitious Catholic. He speaks with a very thick accent. His wife, 'Aunt Elise,' is also short and speaks almost no English. Hers is a more mimed or vaudevillian performance. They clearly love Hansel but they are old and tired and out-of-their-element in 1970s America.*

UNCLE *(and all, getting to the table. Polish accent)*. We sit! Do you want the? Yes, please bring it. We say grace...Thank you God for bringing us out of danger and giving us a new home, though we miss our friends and family who died horribly in the old country. *(Uncle and Aunt cross themselves. Han is clearly uncomfortable with the endless oppressiveness of it, but soldiers on.)* Hansel, we think... *(pronounced "Vee Tink")*
HAN. What?
UNCLE. We think that you are spending too much time with the Vader girl.

HAN. You mean Princess?
UNCLE. Ja, the princess. Hansel, there is no easy way to tell you da truth.
HAN. Truth? What, you don't like her? I know that.
UNCLE. *(Pauses, looks to his wife, then blurts out)* We think she's a vitch!
HAN. *(misses his meaning)* Yeah, she's pain alright.

STAGE RIGHT - NANA'S HOUSE

*(As the lights come up on Nana's home, we see a small but well-appointed living room. Nana is sitting and knitting by a small table on what looks like expensive early 20th c. European chairs. The scene will now play out with characters in a "QUICK-CUT" style dialog between the two groups: HAN, UNCLE, AUNT STAGE LEFT, and PRINCESS and NANA STAGE RIGHT.)*

PRINCESS *(enters)*. Hi Nana!
NANA. How are you miene schatzi? Oh, how pretty your dress *(Princess turns coquettishly to model her skirt in appreciation)*. Ach, look at your figure - you are coming into full bloom! The boys will be crazy for you!
PRINCESS. Oh, you're so bad, Nana! *(both laughing, giggling)*

UNCLE. No, Hansel, A vitch! A succubus!
HAN. Oh, come on, Uncle. You know I don't believe that old-world religious stuff. I mean. You know, now there are all kinds of religions, not just Lutheran. I mean, there's Indian, Chinese... all kinds.
UNCLE. Oh, no, no, Hansel! Vee don't tink dis vay. Life vas so hard for us., all we had was our faith. First the Nazis, den du Stalinists. They all want to kill us, because we were Catholic. We barely escaped to this blessed country to start a new life.
HAN *(depressed)*. Yeah...
UNCLE. You know what happened to your parents. They were betrayed to the Stalinists by fellow Pols. Our countrymen. Ah, the shame of it. *(HAN sighs.)*

*(During the 'Djiouwaski' scene, Nana has brought out

*tea, and Princess has pulled from the crystal-doored cupboard a container containing expensive petite fours and tea cookies. It is a decorated tin container, clearly marked with european art deco ad-designs, a la Alphonse Mucha, and very chic.)*

PRINCESS. What was grandfather like?
NANA. Oh, he was a handsome man... so mysterious... He disappeared, you know, I never saw him after the war.
PRINCESS. Was he like Dad?
NANA. Like your father? Oh, a little. But.. ich weiss nicht. Your father... Ach.. I love him, but he is a wunder dumbkofp so much.
PRINCESS. I know... he's really.. embarrassing.
NANA. Oh, schatzi, all boys are a little stupid. We have to help them along...Don't worry, you'll marry a politician - a very smart man. No dumbkopf for you!
PRINCESS *(sips her tea, thinking).* So...Grandpa was a solider?
NANA. Ja, ja. I think so. Or a spy. It was the war - we never knew exactly who anyone was!

UNCLE. We never knew who anyone was!

PRINCESS. It must have been dangerous!

NANA. It vas! Dangerous. And exciting! I was a dancer, you know! *(Nana gets up and does a little bit of the Charleston playfully, giving a hint of her figure and attractiveness at her prime. Princess laughs and claps enthusiastically)* Ah! Such fun!

UNCLE. Such misery!

PRINCESS. How did you survive?

UNCLE. We had to hide in the forest.

NANA. Oh, you pretended!

UNCLE. It was a time of endless darkness for us! We were forbidden everywhere from practicing our faith!

NANA. Oh! Well, yes, if you wore your heart on your sleeve.

UNCLE. But we refused to back down!

NANA. Like all those stupid Catholic Pollacks!

UNCLE. You can't deny your faith! It makes you who you are!

NANA. Why couldn't they just convert? Just for a few years?

UNCLE. We couldn't hide. What were we supposed to do? Dance for the Nazis?

NANA. We couldn't worry about politics! We would dance for all da soldiers and have such fun! We didn't discriminate - Nazi, Allies -- at our cabaret, we all got along!

UNCLE. Most of the soldiers were just children, teenagers with guns! They didn't know anything about Hitler!

NANA *(Nana settles into the couch).* They weren't all bad, you know. Most were just children, silly teenagers, they didn't know anything about Hitler.
PRINCESS. Was grandfather...?
NANA. Oh...I never asked. He was a soldier. Or a spy. I don't know who he served. Ach, ja. We all have to pay somebody. But, he gave me your papa - who gave me you *(pinching her cheek).*

UNCLE. When our parents - your grandparents - were killed by the Nazis, your momma and papa, miene poor brother, we fled to Russia. And...oh, it's too horrible to say. *(Uncle crosses himself. Aunt Elise buries her head in her hands.)* They died in the gulag. But.. we snuck you out, and brought you to America with us. *(Han lowers his head and rubs his temples. He's heard this story too many times... it's upsetting, he knows it's true, but he can't hear it anymore.)*

16

We just worry for you. Der ist evil in der world, Hansel... just because she is pretty in the face, don't be deceived.
AUNT ELISE *(takes Han's hand in both of hers and looks directly at him).* Mein good *chłopak ("boy" in Polish).* You are good. We love. We love.

NANA. Oh, mien Schatz.. mien Liebling, don't be too anxious to meet the boy. Life is full of boys. Und you, you are so zmart! You have a future, a future we never dreamed of. The whole vorld is yours - if you work for it. If you work hard. And have fun!
PRINCESS. Nana, you're my hero *(hugging her).*

*(The 'JAWASKIs' eat in quiet.)*

HAN. I know it was hard, but...things are better now. You know I'll always take care of you, you and Tante Elise.
UNCLE. *(patting Han's hand, emotional)* We know, Hansel. You are a good boy. We are proud of you.

### SCENE 7

LUKE'S HOUSE - NIGHT

*Twilight. Night is descending in blue-violet and purple. Inside Luke's house, he enters and throws his backpack on kitchen table. Eats something sitting on counter. On the counter sits chopsticks and a bag from "BOBA PHETT's CURRY PALACE".*
*Luke considers, then decides to go to the closet door, with a certain pain and consternation. He sighs heavily. shakes his head. He opens the door with a key.*
*It's an aluminum-foil lined room, with a sky-lights and glowing overhead lamps, filled with a hundred and fifty large cannabis plants. Luke reaches for a hose and takes it in hand, turns the handle and begins watering, shaking his head, clearly unhappy.*
*This scene is played out in silhouette, behind a white screen, with cannabis plants or plant designs projected or shadow-cast onto the screen. The hose can be a pneumatic air hose with a streamer attached at the end for the water/*

*saber effect. We hear rousing 'Star Wars' themed music.*
*Luke does his Tae-Kwan-Do moves with the hose as he waters the pants in a dance both angry and serene, as he does battle with his nemesis – his mother's garden.*
*Lights down.*

### END OF ACT ONE

# ACT TWO

## SCENE 1

LUKE'S HOUSE - DAY

*Aimiee, in a skimpy bikini top and cutoff shorts, with a cigarette and holstered gun, smiles as Han is lifting a big, heavy bale of cannabis 'hay' into the van.*

HAN. Hi Aimiee, How's Business?
AIMIEE'S. I should be asking you.
HAN. It's alright. They pay pretty good for this stuff.
AIMIEE. You know I grow the best. 100% all natural, no preservatives.
HAN. Yeah, It's Chewy here's favorite. He can't get enough.
AIMIEE. You know my secret? It's the soil - I compost my own. I have great worms. You should see their castings. I feed them hemp seeds.
HAN. Worms? Wow, I didn't realize there was so much to it.
AIMIEE. Oh, it's a real art. *(conversational, curious)* Han, where do you hide this stuff? You don't just drive around like that?
*HAN (Han leans in, playful but not serious).* Aimiee, if you wanted to know that, you'd have to get in bed with me.
AIMIEE. Hansel! Why you saucy boy! *(then)* Oh! You hide it under the bed. Is that some kind of.. compartment under there?
HAN. No! No....Yeah. But, don't tell anybody.
AIMIEE. Han, you're secret is my secret. We're in business, doll, and I know how to do business. *(Han finishes the packing, locks up truck.)*
AIMIEE. Say hi to your aunt and uncle. I know how they worry about you.
HAN. You bet. See ya in two weeks.

## SCENE 2

### MAIN STREET / THE VAN

*Han and Chewey are driving down Main Street. Princess is walking on her way back from shopping. The van pulls alongside, upstage of her, but she keeps walking. Han tries to talk to her, while driving and keeping pace with her. It's probably not the first time they've done this.*

HAN. I'm going to Mo's...wanna come?
PRINCESS. With you? *(Han doesn't respond. But he fidgets in his seat as though he's a little uncomfortable.)* Fine. Anything to get out of town.

*(The van stops and Princess hops in. Then the van turns around, revealing the inside – a tricked out swingers pad with a bed, stereo, shag carpet, and mood lighting. Princess sits on the bed and Han keeps driving. She has a thought, then starts looking feverishly through a pile of cassette tapes. She's suddenly very anxious.)*

PRINCESS. Hey....This isn't funny. Where is the tape?
HAN. What tape?
PRINCESS. You know, the tape.
HAN. You can listen to anything. There's a ton of tapes back there. Just grab one.
PRINCESS. No. The "special" tape we made last week...

### SCENE 2-A

### THE VAN (FLASHBACK)

*Han is on the bed. Princess is leaning over him, or straddling him. They're groping and necking. Princess sits up and drops a cassette tape into the stereo. She clicks two buttons at the same time, starting to record. Han reaches up and hits "stop".*

HAN. What're you doing?

PRINCESS. I want to record it. So we can listen to it later. Or when you're not around.
HAN. What? You're crazy.
PRINCESS. Relax, it'll be fun. My dad makes them all the time. *(Han looks at her very, very puzzled.)* Uh, with my MOM. You know how weird they are. Come on, relax, it'll be fun... *(Princess presses the tape, and unbuttons her top and kisses him. Han is bewildered, but he just goes with it.)*

END FLASHBACK. BACK TO THE VAN.

PRINCESS *(suddenly blanches)* Oh my God. I think it was my dad.
HAN. What? How? *(even more astonished)* WHAT?
PRINCESS. I don't know! He just...knows!

THE VAN GOES DARK. CENTER STAGE ILLUMINATES REVEALING -


SCENE 2-B

VADER'S STUDY (FLASHBACK) - NIGHT

*Dr. Vader stands in a towering pose, light from behind and speaking in a deep, booming voice, with a false 'echo' effect - like the Wizard of Oz or Darth Vader.*

DR. VADER. Did you make a sex tape? *(Princess is now cowering before him. She doesn't reply.)*
DR. VADER. Did you make a sex tape?!
PRINCESS. Ewwww. Why would you even ask me that?
DR. VADER. It's a simple question. Did you make a sex tape? *(Princess is squirming. Then, louder, more pressing)* Did you make a sex tape?!
PRINCESS. YES! I DID!!
*(Dr. Don Vader steps out of the shadows and seems a bit more human. Could be staged on a dolly so that he glides in dramatically. He is a large man with a normal, if deep and self-important, voice. He has the drive of a 15 year old but the reduced stamina of a older married guy.)*
DR. VADER. Well, I am very disappointed in you! Why

would you do something like that!
PRINCESS. *(winding up in anger).* GOD! You're such a ... uugghh! *(glances around the room, making sure he can follow her head and eye movements).* Where do you think I got the idea? *(storming out, as she walks away she throws back)* Pervert! *(Dr. Vader looks at his tape collection, and the egg crates on the wall for soundproofing. He leans in and makes sure that the sound-proofing is covering the whole wall, then realizes there is nothing covering the door.)*
DR. VADER. Shit!!! Shit. Shit. Shit. They told me this was soundproof! *(goes to the closet, pulls out a roll of sound-proofing and starts to put it on the door)* Stupid. Shit!

CENTER STAGE GOES DARK. END FLASHBACK.

STAGE RIGHT - INTERIOR VAN *(continuing)*

PRINCESS. Shit. He just knows.
HAN. He hates me.
PRINCESS. Yeah, he does. *(thinking)* You're a lot like him, you know.
HAN *(Tense. Shakes his head).* I can't think about that now. We'll figure it out later, don't worry.
PRINCESS. Shut up.

## SCENE 3-A

MO'S ISLAND TRUCK STOP

*Scenes 3-A to 3-C take place at Moe's Island Truckstop, in the exterior and interiors.*

*They arrive at Mo's Island Truck Stop, a transportation hub where every species of human intermingle and refuel -- 50s greasers in classic cars, bikers, hippies in VW bus, Marines in a jeep, families in campers, rednecks, Elvis impersonators, senior tourists on bus. The van comes to a stop. Chewey jumps out and goes to the back of the van with the bale, doing something to it.*

Princess gets out of van and walks inside - STAGE LEFT.
PRINCESS. I'm getting a Coke.
HAN. Make it last 15 minutes.
PRINCESS. Okay, Mr. Underworld Drug Dealer.
HAN. I'm not a drug dealer. I'm a package delivery service. *(or "this is a package delivery service")*
PRINCESS. *(walking away).* Ha!

*GUIDO approaches. bright but streetwise with a few big pimples and greasy hair, in a t-shirt that's a size too small, with an American Graffiti emblem. He's eating a hoagie that's almost too big for his hand. Han sees Guido, they shake hands in a complex ritual, including a fist bump and a pull-away snap.)*

HAN. Let's do this.

*(Han pulls the wrapped bundles out of the back of the 'falcon' moving efficiently; he hands the packages one by one to Guido, as they occasionally glance around for the cops. GUIDO places them in a duffel bag, and then counts them.)*

GUIDO *(counting carefully, slowly, watching the horizon from time to time).* One, two, three, four... and a half? Mr. Jabah's not gonna be happy about this. You're light again - where does this stuff go, Han? Are you selling it on the side?
HAN. No! No. I don't sell, that's not... I don't sell. I don't know what's happening to...- *(then, loudly)* Hey! *(spying Chewey eating leaves from the package.)* No, Chewey - that's already paid for! *(Han hangs his head, understanding what's been happening. Guido shakes his head in appreciation for the problem.)*
GUIDO. Man... you're one special kind of fuck up, amigo. *(Takes a bite of his large sandwich, and with a mouth full of food, seems to exude a small smile as he realizes he's going to say something he thinks is clever and funny)* "Forget about it, Han... *(dramatically)* It's Chinatown!"

*(Han wrinkles his forehead and scowls - he backs up, as*

*though Guido just challenged him to a fight. Guido tenses up in response to Han's scowl. Suddenly anxious, Guido holds his sandwich pointing slightly at Han. Han makes a false start, shifts his weight back, then, reconsidering, quickly JABS Guido in the jaw. Guido, reels back, shakes his head, and puts his arms up.)*

    GUIDO. Man! What the..?! I didn't even hit you, loco!
    HAN. You were going to!

*(Han points at Guido, still startled - mostly by his own actions, and then backs off. Guido shakes his head, as though in disappointment with what a screw up Han is. He rubs his chin - it wasn't a hard punch.)*

    GUIDO. It's from a movie, dude. "Chinatown?"

*(Han shakes his head, raises his shoulders in an "I don't know" gesture. Or, and alternate dialogue - HAN. Movie!? Who goes to the movies? Guido goes back to eating his sandwich, shaking his head.)*

    GUIDO. One very special kind of fuck-up, man. Jabah's gonna give you a hard time - and I ain't gonna stop him this time...
    HAN *(stands there, looks at Chewey, who is eating cannabis leaves. He hangs his head, exasperated)*. Ssssh...it.

## SCENE 3-B

INSIDE MO'S – THE BAR

*CHARLES CULSHAW CARRINGTON III, aka "C3", 20s, gold-lamé wearing, big afro with gold cape, shorts, sunglasses and roller-skates, a grooved-out, psychedelic 70s roller-dude from London of African descent, C3 is playing a pinball machine, and having a psychedelic experience. He paddles, and rubs and boogies with the machine. The "R2" pinball machine whistles musically.)*
    C3. Chirp for me, baby!

(Across the bar, the mysterious GEORGE is watching C3, Chewey and the others, sipping a coke and writing on his notepad.
Nearby, Chewey is talking with a guy who looks like him, but shorter. They are speaking the same "language", but the short one sounds like Cheech Marin.)

CHEWEY. Arrrgmm Murrur.
SHORT AZTEC. Uhhhhrr. Yeahhh.
CHEWEY. GRuummm Ruurrmmr. *(The fellow Aztec hands Chewey a brightly colored knit pouch - some kind of cheezy Native American tourist souvenir which is full of peyote.)*
SHORT AZTEC. OOOkkkkaaayyyy. Here's the peyote, brother....But, man, you're eating too much ganja, I can barely understand you!

*(Han has walked into Mo's. He looks around for Princess, who's at the bar having a soda. He acknowledges her, and looks around for Chewey. A fairly tall woman with a late 50s hairdo walks up to him. It's MAUREEN "MO" ISLEY, co-owner of the truck stop. She is brash and tough and not afraid to stand up to any of her surly customers.)*

HAN. Hey, Mo.
MO. Hey, Handsome. What brings you to our side of town, sweet cheeks. Oh, never mind *(she puts a hand on his forearm)* - I don't want to know. You bring that little girl with you? Vader's kid. One of 'em, anyway. Listen, when you're looking for something all grown up, you give ol' Mo a call...
HAN. *(playing along)* Alright, Mo... Hey, you seen Chewey?
MO. He's right over there, talking to those Indians.
HAN. Catch ya later...*(Han walks to Chewey, gives a 'hey, let's get going' pat.)*

## SCENE 3-C

MO'S ISLAND, PARKING LOT

*Extras in various dress, cross the parking lot at this busy truck stop, including George. C3 rolls by on roller skates over to the van as Han and Princess, Chewey are getting in.*

C3. Yo, Han. Can a brother get a lift?
HAN. Hey, C3. I'm going back to town, but the van's kinda full.
C3. I can dig it. Any chance we can do a little fender bender?
HAN. I'll keep it under 40.

*(Han jumps in the van. C3 hits play on his portable 8-track player and sits on the rear bumper.*
*MUSIC BLASTS. "HOOKED ON CLASSICS, BEETHOVEN'S 9TH", as the van speeds off. C3 is jamming, rocking out with those giant golden headphones.)*


## SCENE 4

MAIN STREET

*When the van comes into town, C3 holds onto the back and skate-dances down Main St. They pass Sheriff Tigh's Interceptor and C3 waves. Tigh just shakes his head. C3 lets go of the bumper and continues on.)*

C3. Stay cool, baby!

*(The van parks in the empty lot and Chewey gets out.)*
CHEWEY. (teasing) Arrumph ahh ahh.
HAN. Shut up. I'll see you tomorrow.
*(Chewey and Han turn the van around, revealing the inside, and Chewey exits. Han crawls onto the bed with Princess who is waiting for him. Han leans in, kisses her, she pulls him close, hands, clothes, lips move about in a frenzy.)*

HAN. *(jumps back, waving his hand)* Ouch! *(re: her star of David necklace)* Why don't you take that damn thing off? It pokes me every time. Why do you wear that, it's like a 'star of death'.

PRINCESS. It was from my Nana for my bat mitzvah.

HAN. *(puzzled)* Is that a European thing? *(Princess scowls.)* Wait, was that from senior year? you know I had to drop out to help my uncle run the yard.

PRINCESS *(She looks at him with growing disgust, shaking her head).* Don't talk. You'll only make it worse.

LIGHTS FADE DOWN


SCENE 5

DAY GO BAR & DINER - DAY

*Ben is perched on his stool with Luke is happily sipping his milk beside.*

LUKE. She's sooo beautiful. Don't you think so?

BEN. She's alright, if you're into that sort of thing. *(takes a drink)*

LUKE. I mean it Ben. I really her. She's just... there's something so different about her.

BEN. Her mother was a looker too, before HE got a hold of her. Turns gold into doo-doo. Like King Midas in reverse...

LUKE. I mean it Uncle Ben. I really think she could be 'the one.' Sometimes I just stare at her, and - she looks back - and I know she feels it too. It's like.. there's a connection. It's chemical.

BEN. Okay, kid, you're scaring me. Listen, she may have nice little boobies, but look at where she comes from. *(pauses, looks at Luke)* Her father? I mean, Luke, let's face it, that guy is a piece of work. Screwing everybody in town. Everybody, Luke EVV-REE-BODY.

LUKE *(not taking the hint).* What do you have against him? What'd he do to you?

BEN. Plenty, Luke. Plenty. *(Ben sips his bourbon, stares into the distance.)*

LUKE. Oh, darn it! I've got to go! I've got to pick up some moisture vaporators for my mother's stupid plants!

*(Luke runs out of the diner, throwing his backpack over his shoulders and running home. Ben sips his drink, and looks into the glass. Bens voice continues to echo -- "Plenty.... plenty... plenty." We hear MORTAR EXPLOSIONS and GUNFIRE. LIGHTS DOWN and UP, GOING RED and YELLOW)*

SCENE 6

FLASHBACK - KOREA - 1952 - FOXHOLE

*A much younger Sargent Ben is huddled close to 19 year old Private Vader in the pitch black, trying to keep their wits as the artillery rips through the darkness.*

BEN. Korea, what a dump! I never thought I'd miss Barstow...
VADER. Oh, it's got its charms. I kind of like Asia, actually. Surprisingly so... But, I'll have to get back eventually.
BEN. What do you wanna do when you get home?
VADER. Well, first there's medical school. I'll probably specialize in something worthwhile, something that'll make a difference in people's lives.
BEN. Oh, that's nice.
VADER. As long as it's lucrative. I'm going to have to marry money or earn it. Probably both. Probably both...
BEN. I was thinking of opening a bar - right downtown. Right in the middle of Main Street. Easy to find. Open all day, a place where the guys can go and relax, wet their whistle, just have some "man time" away from all the stress.
VADER. That sounds nice, Ben. I'll visit you in your bar when I'm not busy.. I'm going to run for office, you know.
BEN. Really? Politics? Oh.. I didn't know. You're built for it, though. Big, handsome...
VADER. I think if I play my cards right, I could be a big man in the republican party. In time, a powerful man...
BEN. Like a councilman?

VADER. No... think bigger.
BEN. Congressman?
VADER. No... think bigger.
BEN. I'm thinking
VADER. Even bigger..
BEN. I'm right there, Don. Right there.
VADER. Exactly. Vice-President.
BEN. Oh.
VADER. Oh, is yes. The man who really has all the power - the man who pulls the strings. VP. I can do it. I think I can really do it.
BEN. I ... I think you can, too, Don. I believe in you. Hell, I might even vote for ya, with that charm. Even though I always vote democrat. And it would kill mother...

*(BOOM)*

BEN. Oh, Don.
VADER. Ben! BEN! I can't die here. I can't go like this! There is so much I have to do in this world!
BEN. I know! I know, Don... I know!

*(BOOM! B-A-B-O-O-O-M! Vader and Ben are blown over by the blast, onto each other.)*

BEN *(dazed)*. Oh, Oh, are you alright.
VADER. Yea, yes. I'm okay..
BEN. Don, if this is it. I just wanted to say...
VADER. I know Ben, I know. You don't have to say it. It would... make me uncomfortable. but I know. And I am flattered. And at a different time, in a different place, if one of us had a vagina...
BEN. Oh..So you never...?
VADER. No. You mean have I?
BEN. Yeah, No. I mean, ever wanted to?
VADER. Oh, come on.

*(BOOM!! Shrapnel and debris rip through the air.)*

VADER. Well.

*(BOOM!!)*

VADER. I mean.

(BOOOMMMM!)

VADER. Okay! I've thought about it.
BEN. What?
VADER. Come on, before I change my mind. Just one thing - if we do this... I'm the man!
BEN. Donald Vader, I wouldn't have it any other way.

(LIGHTS DOWN. *The shelling continues dramatically, fading into the distance.*

    BOOM!
       BOOM!
          BOOM!)

## SCENE 7

### BOBA PHETT'S CURRY PALACE

*The inside of the restaurant is brightly colored in saffrons, reds and yellow featuring a large dancing Shiva statue, a huge fishtank, and an elephant motif. It's very modes, with there are silks or streamers to brighten it up.*

*Han and Chewey are eating at a shabby old red vinyl booth was bought second-hand from a defunct 50s diner.*

HAN. I just don't think she understands me.
CHEWEY. Rurrurrghmm.
HAN. I mean.. she always seems.. mad. Like.. I did something wrong.
CHEWEY. Murrgh.
HAN. I don't know... I don't know what I'm doing with her. My aunt and uncle don't like her...they think she's a .. vitch. (Priya enters from the kitchen in a traditional sari) Oh, Hey Priya.
PRIYA. How is everything Han, Chewey?
CHEWEY. GRRMMRUGH
HAN. Yeah, it's always good. You know we can't stay

away.
　　PRIYA. Oh, you are so kind to support our restaurant. My parents are very fond of you. You always bring us luck.
　　HAN. What? How?
　　PRIYA. You always bring us new customers, those men you deliver parcels for. They always eat so many different plates!
　　HAN. Oh, yeah.. Jabah and his ... guys. Well, it's nothing, Pri. You're too nice to us - tell you the truth, we're just a couple of scoundrels.
　　PRIYA. Oh, no! Don't try that line on me - I know you, Hansel Djiouwaski - you honor your aunt and uncle, you are always working, and you never complain. You are a good man.
　　HAN. Well... I.. .don't know what to say. I'm...
　　CHEWEY. GRROOORMMR!
　　DJANGO. If it isn't our good luck charms - Han and Chewey. Priya, leave them alone to eat in peace! Help me in the kitchen. These potatoes can't cook themselves.
　　PRIYA. Coming papa. *(to Han and Chewey)* Enjoy your meal.
　　HAN. Priya?
　　PRIYA. Yes?
　　HAN. Uh.. thanks. *(Priya smiles and walks away)*
　　CHEWEY. AARUGGUGGMM
　　HAN. Come on, buddy. A girl like that would never go for a guy like me.
　　CHEWEY. Ar Ar ARaaggmm *(laughing because that's precisely what is happening. Priya stops at the kitchen door, looks back and smiles, before exiting. The two continue to eat in a moment of silence).*
　　PRINCESS *(bursting through the door.)* Hey, Losers! Let's go! *(Han and Chewey look up, surprised. They continue to respond with looks of slight confusion and continue to slowly chew their food as she speaks.)* We've got to GO! The party? *(Han looks up from eating, with a raised eyebrow look of "I don't know" on his face.)* The party. The tape? Our Plan? That's tonight!
　　HAN *(slowly remembering.)* Oh...yeeaah *(drawn out)*. I guess we'll take this to go...

31

# SCENE 8

## THE KEY PARTY. DR. VADER'S HOUSE

*This scene takes place in Dr. Vader's home which has multiple isolatable areas of action and will require careful staging. They are:*
*Front of the House (Exterior)*
*Living Room*
*Hallway*
*Dr. Vader's Study*
*Princess' Bedroom*
*Master Bedroom*

*We start inside the van, with Han, Chewey and Princess. They drive past the front of Vader's house just as PARTY GUESTS arrive at the front door.*

PRINCESS. Not here, dummy - park down the block!
HAN. Okay, Princess! Take it easy! *(mumbles to himself)* don't be such a vitch.

*(The van drives off stage and we focus on the front of the house, where any and all town dignitaries and stepford couples are in their best dress outfits approaching the house. We see on the mailbox "Dr. Vader and family" and a sign on the outside, "Dr. Don Vader, ObGyn, Proctologist, appointment or drop-in" and a phone number. Mrs Vader opens the front door to greet people.)*

CANDY. Hi Tom, Hi Viv. Hi Jack...(Nicholson), Warren (Beaty), Diane (Keaton), Hi Carly (Simon).

## VADER'S STUDY

*The same room where he fought with Princess earlier. We enter a darkened room, where Don is standing in his robe, which he's wearing over his dress clothes; his arm is raised, his forearm extended. There is a falcon on it - On two visible walls are large glowing posters - images of Richard Nixon and Henry Kissinger. They seem almost alive.)*

DR. VADER. .. That's right, Admiral Akbar, Tonight we hunt.

LIVING ROOM

*Mrs. Vader has stepped inside -- the facade of the house has flown up/off. As the guests enter they each drop something into a giant fishbowl. CPO3 enters, and Mrs. Vader is very pleased to see him.*

CANDY. Hello Charles.
C3. Hello Candy. You look fine tonight.
CANDY. *(blushes and thrusts forward the bowl full of keys.)* I need your keys, please.
C3. *(smiles deep into her eyes, then places an oversized gold skeleton key it into the bowl)* I hope somebody special finds that key.
CANDY. I'm sure she will.
C3. Right on.

STAGE RIGHT - BLACK

*A spotlight hits Princess in a crouched position. She looks behind her into the darkness.*

PRINCESS. Ready? Now stick to the plan. If anyone sees you, just act natural. And Han, do NOT go into my room.
*(Han and Chewey, crouched, shuffle into the light close behind her. They are wearing army-navy camouflaged ponchos and motorcycle goggles.)*
PRINCESS. What're you wearing? You guys are so.. Ugh!

*(They creep UP STAGE and through a door into--)*

HALLWAY

*(They creep down the hallway carefully. Then, a DRUNK GUEST stumbles between them, startling Princess. She grabs Han and jumps in the first open doorway, but Chewey is carried down the hallway to the living room, where a woman grabs his arm and pulls him close.)*

LIVING ROOM

PARTY GIRL #1. Oh, c'mere. *(turned on)* I didn't know this was a costume party.
WARREN. *(pretentiously)* So, I went down to Escondito to see the total eclipse of the sun.
CARLY. UGH... Jesus, you're so... vain.

PRINCESS' BEDROOM

*(The lights come up on Princess's bedroom. Princess listens at the door waiting for the hallway to clear. But Han starts looking around -- not taking the "mission" very seriously. Going through her stuff he finds awards, family memorabilia, which all have some reference to Judaism and Israel. He reads a plaque aloud.)*

HAN. Princess Leah Vader... Leah? Lee-ah? *(laughs)* What kind of name is that? *(Reading aloud)* Bat. Mit...z... vah. *(re: another plaque, reading slowly).* Is-ra-els 25th birthday? *(he looks at her and then the pictures and slowly asks)* Is your family... Yiddish?
PRINCESS *(with utter pitying disgust)* UUUGGH. Moron. We have to get into the study.
*(She opens the door and they sneak, tiptoe across the empty hallway, and through another door into darkness.)*

LIVING ROOM

*(Dr. Vader enters in a colorful 70s swingers outfit, tight polyester, long collar, and holding a giant brandy sifter. He's the man on the scene - and we see him pulling girls to him, laughing uproariously at his own glee and sexual gluttony. The guests are increasing in their excitement as they gather around the giant fishbowl containing all the keys. We see Candy Vader sets the fishbowl on a pedestal, but coyly pulls out the golden key of CPO3, and tucks it into her pink Chanel suit without anyone but the audience noticing. She's chosen him already.)*

DR. VADER. Let the ceremony begin!

VADER'S STUDY

*(Princess and Han have made it into the study, Nixon and Kissinger glow. As the lights come up, we see for the first time in this room, an edifice like a series of stacked polygons - stark white and black shapes across the horizon, like the surface of some great edifice -- it is a giant mid-century styled case full of reel to reel tapes. Princess begins shuffling through it. Han wanders about the room a bit aimlessly, taking it all in. This is Vader's conquest room. In the corner is an oversized, flat couch -- a leather futon with a fake fur comforter. There's a huge Hi-Fi and the walls are covered in soundproofing foam. A groovy and sleazy man cave.)*

PRINCESS. No, no, it's not here. These are all reel-to-reel.
HAN. What is all this stuff?
PRINCESS. Don't ask, my dad is a total perv.

LIVING ROOM

*(Don Vader, master of ceremonies, holds up the fishbowl of keys dramatically and waxes poetically in a speech that is completely over the top, but he's serious--)*

DR. VADER. When the great Bacchus flew on the mighty golden chariot of Aasgard, and the many winged griffin flew down from Helm's Deep...then Aphrodite's passion burned with a heat brighter than the many suns of Isis...

VADER'S STUDY

*(Princess continues searching frantically. Han is distracted by items in the room.)*

HAN. I think that poster just... looked at me. Is this *(examining it)*...glass? It's like a TV screen....from the future!
PRINCESS *(desperate)* Would you please help me look, please!?
HAN. Is this one of those Andy Warhol things?

PRINCESS. It's not here!

*(Suddenly a noise at the door, and a couple backs in, laughing, groping, kissing in a mad fury of polyester. Han and Princess look at each other and dive under the couch. She shoves him into the corner, in abrasive whispers.)*

PRINCESS. Move Over! *(pause)* Over!
HAN *(loud whisper)*. I'm stuck! *(she hits him)* Ow!

*(DON VADER and NAOMI, blonde with long legs and very large breasts, fall down onto the couch with peals of laughter. Princess and Han squirm underneath. As the swingers make out Han is getting a little turned on and motions to Princess, who rebuffs his advances with disgust and hitting. She shakes her head.)*

DR. VADER. You know, you're a very special girl, Naomi. Very, very, very.
NAOMI. I've heard big things about you, Don. *(The Kissinger poster's eyes seem to light up.)*
DR. VADER. Very... Big things. *(Big ZIPPER sound effect.)*
NAOMI. Oh! Ohhh. Oh!

CANDY'S BEDROOM

*(C3 and Candy are making love in bed. He's behind her, with the sheets covering the naughty bits. It's heavy and passionate.)*

C3. That's it baby bird! Chirp for daddy! *(Candy makes a tweeting R2D2 series of chirps, moans and whistles.)*

VADER'S STUDY

DR. VADER. Oh. Oh! Oh! Oooh! Ooh ooh.
NAOMI. Ow. Ow! Ouch.. ouchh. OUCH! Ow.
PRINCESS *(under the bed, stone-faced, trying not to listen)*. I can't believe this is happening... Again. *(Han shoots her a look, "What??" She sighs, exasperated.)*

HALLWAY

*(A door opens and Chewey emerges, smiling, with his goggle askew, groaning a light happy sound, knees a little weak. A pair of hands grab him from behind.)*

PARTY GIRL #1. Ohh, Chewey, honey, don't leave.
PARTY GIRL #2. We're just getting started, monkey man.. *(A second set of hands wraps around his waist and pulls him back in. The door slams shut to the GIGGLES of the girls. Chewey MOANS with delight.)*
CHEWEY. Grrrwrrrrooroo!

VADER'S STUDY

*(Post-Coitus. Vader sits on the edge of the bed, his feet inches from Princess' face. Naomi pulls up her skirt and starts buttoning her blouse, not listening to him.)*

DR. VADER. And my daughter doesn't understand me. She thinks I'm the worst person in the world. Worse than Hitler! Can you believe that? I've bought her so many, many things! What did Hitler ever buy for anybody? Nothing!
NAOMI. Yeaaahhh....well. Thanks... Don. That was....interesting. You truly are the "Biggest in Barstow." But you know, there is this little thing called... "foreplay?"

*(He looks confused as she walks out and closes the door. Dr. Vader shrugs off the insult then reaches behind the headboard and pulls out a CB radio-style recording microphone for the reel-to-reel recorder.)*

DR. VADER. *(into the mic)* Nay-oohh-mi...Summer party, seven-tee fourrrrrr. Read it and weep. Read it...and weep.

*(Dr. Vader looks up at the Kissinger and Nixon posters, which seem to smile. He sets down the mic, extremely pleased with himself, then gets up in his samurai robe, and goes to the bathroom. He leaves the door open and starts URINATING loudly. Princes pushes Han to get out from under the bed.)*

PRINCESS. Go, go, go!

*(Princess and Han are inching out from under the bed. The PEEING STOPS and they freeze, but the PEEING resumes. Stops, then resumes. Princess is crawling out of her skin, but she can't get caught. They're almost out, when Han stops--)*

HAN. *(loud whisper)* Wait! I lost my goggles.
PRINCESS. *(hard whisper)* Hurry!

*(But it's too late. Vader returns from the bathroom, Princess and Han quickly scurry back under the bed, just in time. Vader sits on the bed/couch and starts chewing on a half-eaten sandwich on a plate by the bed. He chews, completely satisfied with himself. Princess is mortified.)*

DR. VADER. Oh, yes.
PRINCESS. *(low)* Asshole.

END OF ACT TWO

# ACT THREE

## SCENE 1

### STAGE LEFT - MAIN STREET - VACANT LOT

*Han and Chewey tinker under the hood of the van.*

HAN. Hand me the spanner. *(Takes a wrench from Chewey without looking, his head under the hood, then reacts)* No, the spanner!
CHEWEY. Grrrunnrroo.
HAN. No, the other one!
CHEWEY. GROOWMMGG
HAN. Well, I don't know.. Give me that wrench. *(He works for a minute, then)* Chewey, about Princess. Did you know?
CHEWEY. Aru Arg Ar.
HAN. That she was Jewish?
CHEWEY. Brruuaagg.
HAN. You did? Why didn't you tell me?
CHEWEY. URGGG RU.
HAN. Well, how was I supposed to know? She always ate with us. Don't they have to eat special food?
CHEWEY. Arrrrgrugm.
HAN. No, you're right. I don't really care about that. It's just that...
CHEWEY. RUUURURM
HAN. Yeah. she is. A real *vitch*.

## SCENE 2

### VADER'S OFFICE - CENTER STAGE

*Dr. Vader is kneeling on the ground before the image of Nixon, watching, enraptured. The images of NIXON and KISSINGER hang left and right, they seem to glow eerily and flicker, as though they are alive. This effect can be created with actors behind screens, with visual projection or possibly pre-recorded videos. Nixon speaks in a very excited, energetic and even paranoid caricature of the man, a la Nixon on the cartoon "Futurama." Kissinger is understated and dry, but very confidant.)*

    NIXON. DON VADER!
    DR. VADER. Yes, my master.
    NIXON. Don! Don. We needja Don. We needja to be strong out there in California. Hold it. Hold it against the commies in their fancy schools. They wouldn't let me into one of their fancy liberal schools with the pretty girls. Berkeley! Or UCLA! I had to go to Whitier College with the dogfaces. The dogfaces, Don! But I showed them, didn't I? Didn't I, Henry?
    KISSINGER. You did, Mr. President.
    NIXON. Don. Now, listen to me. We need you to hold onto it out there. We can't lose California in '76. We can't lose her, Don. Donoronio! Lord Don!
    DR. VADER. I will be strong, my Lord!
    KISSINGER. May I interrupt, Mrs. President?
    NIXON. What is it, Henry?
    KISSINGER. I think he needs to know.
    NIXON. We're losing Vietnam, Don. We're losing it! Those godless commies. We're fighting on two fronts.
    KISSINGER. Three Mr. President. The Viet Cong, the godless liberals -
    NIXON. And the pinko media, those rat-fuckers! Yes, Henry. Three fronts. That's why we need you, Don-orino, Don-oronio. We need you to hold California. A show of Force! A show of strength, Don. You need to TAKE it. We need you to run for state Senate.
    DR. VADER. You mean?
    NIXON. We're starting you on the path. On the path, Donny boy.
    DR. VADER. My training...Is...is it complete?
    KISSINGER. Our training is never complete, Dr. Vader - it is our lifelong service to our ideals that makes us what we are.
    DR. VADER. Of course...of course.
    NIXON. Take it. Don. If you get a chance to grab the prize - never look back, and don't worry about trampling a few Jews and idiots along the way. If they throw themselves under your steamroller, whose fault is it if they turn into

ground beef?

DR. VADER. Theirs?

NIXON. That's right. That's Right, Don!

DR. VADER. I'm ready... give the word.

NIXON. You're a good boy, Don. Now, go get 'em.

DR. VADER. I...actually have to go get dressed. I have a full roster of patients today. You know - I am a gynecologist.

KISSINGER. And a proctologist.

DR. VADER *(pausing, not entirely happy with the jibe but not wanting to offend Kissinger)*. It pays the bills.

NIXON. Off with you then, son, don't leave her waiting with her legs in the air! *(laughs. Dr. Vader rises with purpose and exits. Nixon and Kissinger watch him go.)*

NIXON. That boy is our last hope.

KISSINGER *(pause, considering)*. No, there is another.

*(LIGHTS DOWN.)*

NIXON. You mean...*(horrified)* The actor?

## SCENE 3

*This scene is comprised of three intercut sub-scenes played across the stage. The energy is ramping up for the County Fair. The action is staged as follows:*

*STAGE RIGHT - Main Street, the Van; Princess, Han, Chewey*
*STAGE LEFT - Day-Glow Bar; Aimiee and Ben*
*CENTER STAGE - Vader's study; Dr. Vader, Admiral Akbar (his falcon)*

*Main St. Barstow is now entirely decorated with POSTERS. "Carnival Tonight! Japanese Samurai Touring Company. First Prize - Real Replica Shogun Helmet"*

STAGE RIGHT - MAIN STREET - THE VAN

*Han and Chewey are standing next to the Falcon, parked outside the beauty salon.*

HAN. We're gonna win that 200 bucks tonight, Chewey. I have a good feeling - and that'll put me in good with Mr. Jabah.
CHEWEY. Rughrr.
HAN. I think it looks great. I don't know what she's talking about.
PRINCESS *(walking up)*. Hey losers! *(Han and Chewey grumble.)*

STAGE LEFT - DAY-GO BAR & DINER

*(Ben and Aimiee are leaning against the wall outside the Day-glow diner, having a smoke; Ben is also sipping a gin and tonic.)*

BEN. So, cuz', you goin' to the fair?
AIMIEE. Honey, I'm gonna work it. That whole samurai pavilion? Total networking opportunity. (*Ben doesn't quite understand, Aimiee just invented the term "networking".)*

CENTER STAGE - VADER'S STUDY

DR. VADER (*standing in his samurai robe in front of Nixon, with his falcon perched on his arm.)* Do you know what tonight is, Admiral? It's the night of the county fair. The night the king of Barstow struts his stuff. Yes, it is...

HAN. You know... I'm getting awfully tired of you calling us 'losers' all the time.
CHEWEY. Arrgh *(in agreement).*
PRINCESS. Who said I was talking to Chewey?
CHEWEY. Arra! arra! Shrrrnnt! *(laugh-growls, but quiets and snorts when Han points at him abruptly).*
HAN. Well, we'll see who's laughing when I win that 200 bucks! Come on, let's get movin'. *(The three start to get into the Falcon, Han takes one last look at the mural, running his hand over the side of the van with care.)*

BEN. Do you think Don will be there?
AIMIEE. HUH! He wouldn't miss it. A chance to show off.
BEN. And he loves that Japanese stuff ever since the war.

DR. VADER. The Japanese touring company is coming to Barstow tonight! This...Is...My test! Just as Henry and Dr. Kissinger said. 1974, the year that the world is introduced to Don Vader!

BEN. He stayed in Japan for a year after Korea. Nobody knows what he was up to..
AIMIEE. Probably a few little 'Dons' running around Osaka.

DR. VADER. I must win the helmet - that is my challenge! The Samurai will embrace me like my adopted mother. JAPAN! Home of compliant, diminutive women and ritual concubinage! (*A giant poster or flag of Japan flies in behind Vader. He is framed within its giant red circle in a field of white.*)

BEN. Well, maybe he shouldn't get everything he wants for a change.

DR. VADER. What this town needs is a show of force! Something they will respect!

AIMIEE. The helmet? You're gonna stop him?

DR VADER. I'll use all my power to take it. Then, and only then they'll know, Admiral. I am their leader.

BEN. Correction. We're gonna stop him.
AIMIEE (*Aimiee takes a drag, then shakes his hand*). Deal.

*STAGE LEFT AND CENTER black out, leaving only--*

SCENE 4

STAGE RIGHT - THE BICENTENNIAL FALCON

*Han, Princess and Chewey are in the van, driving quietly. Princess is ignoring Han, she's mostly done with him. She sees Luke walking along, gi and backpack.*

PRINCESS. Hiiii Luke! Whatcha up to?
LUKE. Hi Princess! Nothing Mom wants me to go to Tashi Hardware and pick up some power converters.
PRINCESS. We're going to eat. Why don't you come?
HAN. No.
PRINCESS. *(ignoring Han)* Han says sure! Get in!

*(Luke jumps in sitting in between Han and Princess, more or less crouching on the gear box looking aw shucks enthusiastic; Han looks irritable, mumbling a little to himself. Chewey seems unbothered, pats Luke on the head.*
*They drive down main street to Boba and Django Phett's Thai-Indian Curry Palace. Inside, it's a big place, almost totally empty. Boba and Django are very happy to see them.)*

## SCENE 5

### BOBA PHETT'S CURRY PALACE

*Han, Chewey, Princess and Luke enter.*

BOBA. Oh, it's our favorite customers.
DJANGO. Han and Chewy and young Lucas - our good luck charms. *(Django sits them at a red vinyl booth and then hurries into the kitchen.)*
PRINCESS *(To Luke)*. I didn't know you knew about this place.
LUKE. Oh, my mom orders from here all the time. She said she heard about it from a friend at work. *(Han has an anxious cough, in response).*
PRINCESS *(making the connection and prodding them a little)*. A friend from work? That's a coincidence. Isn't that how you told me you started coming here?
HAN *(looking at Luke and then back to Princess, trapped)*. What, no, it's not like that...we have a completely professional...
LUKE *(improvising, trying to fill in a story)*. Yeah, Han does shipping for my mom's... hum..

HAN. Medical products.

*(Princess squints at both of them, raising her eyebrows, enjoying making them squirm. Then Priya walks up with some flat bread (naan) and a beer for Han. Han winks a thanks to her, then salutes her with the bottle as he takes a swig.)*

PRIYA. Hello Ms. Vader, Han, Chewey, Luke, what will you have today?

HAN. Oh, the usual all around, Priya. Whatever the special is.

PRIYA. Eggplant Vindaloo with our special secret coconut curry and rice, for everyone. Except, a salad with dressing on the side for Princess *(leaning in slightly with a happy smile)* You see, I remember! *(She takes the menus and exits to the kitchen)*

HAN. Hey, you guys jazzed for the County Fair? The Eagle is gonna win first prize.

Chewey *(enthusiastically)*. ARRRRR!

LUKE. What's the Eagle?

PRINCESS. Oh! You mean the bicentennial FALCON! *(She points and laughs.)*

HAN. No one can tell the difference, only stupid college girls who think they know everything.

LUKE *(NICE, to a fault, always trying to be pleasant, he jumps in to calm the tension)*. Hey, you guys! Come on! Han, I'm sure it's great.

*(The bells rings at the door and TWO SOLDIERS - National Guard or Army, about to be sent to Vietnam - walk in and are seated across the room by Django.)*

PRINCESS *(softly)*. Did you guys here the news? They're sending more troops.

HAN. Hm.

LUKE. I thought about enlisting next year.. I'll be 18. Mom says she needs me, but...Hey, Han.. you're like...20-something. How come you didn't get drafted?

HAN *(drinking)*. Well...*(leaning in)* I don't have a social security number. Because of the way I came into the country.

PRINCESS. In a basket.

HAN. Ha, ha! *(Quietly)* It was a trunk.
LUKE. But don't you want to serve your country?
HAN. Look, I'm all for America, I mean, I'll defend her in a fight. But what'd the Vietnamese ever do to us?
PRINCESS *(Touches Luke's hand. Han notices).* Luke, it's an illegal war.
LUKE. Hm.
PRIYA *(walking up with plates of food).* Oh, it's not the first time an empire has fought to keep a colony and lost.
DJANGO *(from offstage).* PRIYA!
PRIYA. Be right there!
PRINCESS. Think about it, Luke - if someone invaded this country, wouldn't you fight them?
LUKE. Well, I guess I would...
HAN *(Looking at Princess' hand which is still on Luke's. He slaps his hand on top of hers).* Kid, you're a little wound up. What do you want to go to war for? You want to come back messed in the head like Sensei Mike? You'd be better off doing something to relax now and then. *(With free his hand he mimes a 'cigarette' inhale).* Do your head good. *(Han Lifts Princess' hand off of Luke's.)*
LUKE. I don't know. That stuff makes you funny. I need to focus. Clean body. Clean mind. *(He does a few of punching/blocking kung fu moves dramatically. The others share a look, knowing that when they get high together it comes from Luke's mom. Priya approaches with a water pitcher.)*
PRIYA. How is everything? *(They all improvise "Good," "fine" "great" 'arrrarg." Then a LOUD CRASH comes from the Kitchen.)*
DJANGO. *(off-stage, yelling)* POTATOES!
PRIYA. Oh!

*(Priya runs out to help. Han gets up, maybe to help, or just see what's going on. Han walks over, peeks in the kitchen to see if there is a real problem. The others all peer toward the door. At the same time, Chewey, has pulled out his knitted souvenir bag full of Peyote. He looks around and decides with a huge grin to sprinkle it like faerie dust all over the food. Han walks back.)*

HAN. It's fine, they just fell of a shelf. *(Everyone*

continues eating.)
    LUKE. This is really good. I have it all the time - my mom gets it for dinner. And lunch. And, well. A lot. But.
    HAN. It is good.
    PRINCESS. It's really good.
    LUKE. It's like.. I dunno. I wonder what the smecial ingredient is. Ibs Bike a mealy meshmal... *(The others look at him. He's not making sense.)* I feel funny...

    *(Luke leans his head over, groggy, on Princess's shoulder. The LIGHTS CHANGE, a DISCO BALL BURSTS INTO LIGHT and MUSIC SWELLS. He raises his eyes, she looks at him, they begin to make out, stroking each other's face - they fall into each other in a wash of white robes and mini-skirts.*
    *LIGHTS FLASH - MUSIC ENDS ABRUPTLY. Princess is eating as before, but Luke is on the floor, writhing around and groping for an invisible lover. It never happened - he's hallucinating.*
    *The others laugh at Luke WRITHING ON THE FLOOR making out with the air and kissing his hand.*

    *The LIGHTS FLASH and highlight Princess and Han.)*

    PRINCESS. *(turned on)* Oh, yeah...
    HAN. *(confused as a strange feeling takes over his body).* What is happening?

    *(A WHITE LIGHT FLOODS THE ROOM and Princess gets up from the table and dances dramatically to CENTER STAGE where Nymphs or Angels are twisting fabric like clouds. The LIGHTS and DISCO BALL and MUSIC tell us we're in Princess' fantasy -- a city in the clouds -- surrounded by orange-golden light and purple clouds.*
    *Princess climbs 3 steps atop a floating (rolling) cloud. Then a figure appears, a statue, strong, frozen in place and with a giant tongue. It looks like Han.)*

    HAN. Princes, what are we doing? I can't feel my arms.
    PRINCESS. *(cuts him off)* Shhhhhhhhh. *(Princess smiles as her cloud takes her over to the Han stature, where his tongue is in line with her crotch. She grabs the statue, she's*

*in ecstasy.)*
    HAN. Princess... *(muffled)* what're you doing...?
*(Princess plops her miniskirt on his head, and (we imagine) throttles his stiff, half-frozen out-stuck tongue driving herself to orgasm. As Han's muffled protests go unheeded.)*
    VELVETY AFRICAN-AMERICAN VOICE. You truly belong up here with us, among the clouds. *(Princess throws back her hair in pure pleasure.)* You truly belong up here with us, among the clouds.
    PRINCESS: Ahh! Ahhh!! AHHHH!!! YEEESSSS!!! YESSSSS!!! FINALLLLYYYY!!! YESS!!!

*(She climaxes with a sci-fi echo effect. The LIGHTS FLASH, the stage resets and Princess is now back in the booth. She's sitting, head back. Han sees Princess sort of gurgling, her head back, exposing her neck, smiling drunkenly, widely, moaning a bit. Han stands up to leave and crosses the dark stage, stepping into--*

THE BICENTENNIAL FALCON - DREAM VERSION

*Han is in the driver's seat, with Chewey at his side. He looks back to the restaurant, confused, then shakes it off. He puts a cassette in the 8-track and drives. The Falcon speeds along to the MUSIC. TIGH'S INTERCEPTOR pulls alongside in pursuit, hits the LIGHTS and SIREN. Han feels the thrill of the chase. He hits the gas to the floor. The chase is on. He looks back and sees Chewey, Princess and Luke all smoking pot and laughing. No one is worried.*
    *The Interceptor catches up to the Falcon and gets neck in neck with Han.)*

    SHERIFF TIGH. You can't outrun me, Jewiski!
    HAN *(looking to his left, then forward, then left, then back to the dash)*. Okay Chewey, hit it!!

*(Chewey throws a switch and the van lights up. Han looks to Tigh, laughs and gives him the bird. Then he grabs the throttle, yanks it back and something HUMMS into high WHIRRR. The van shakes, rocks, at high speed. Tigh smirks. He's got Han again.*

*Inside the van, the cockpit is aglow with lights flashing on Han's face. Then the lights and stars in the sky stretch into long threads. Han, Princess, Chewey and Luke are all amazed.*

*Lights shoot out into the audience, smoke, SFX climax, then – POOF – the van disappears and with a SCREACH, THE BICENTENNIAL FALCON zooms overhead (as a model) crossing the night sky.)*

HAN. Yaaaa HOOOOOOO!!!!!"

*(Tigh gets out of his car and watches in humiliation as the Falcon escapes.)*

*LIGHT CHANGE and we're back to Boba's, revealing Han laying on the floor beside the table. He only made it a few steps. Chewey looks at his hallucinating friends and takes a sip from his coke, not surprised.)*

CHEWEY. *(in English)* Wow. You guys are really wasted.


## SCENE 6

### THE BARSTOW COUNTY FAIR

*The next 4 sub-scenes all take place at the county fair.*
*Fairgrounds*
*Water-pistol booth*
*Helmet Battle*
*Ben and Don Confrontation*

*The Barstow county fair is a classic rural fair with carnival rides, games, balloons, food stands, tents, a classic car show, and the featured event -- the Nakamuri traveling Samurai exhibit. We should see lots of lights, balloons and exciting amusements. Everyone from town is at the fair. All available non-featured cast should roam through these scenes as extras.*

GUIDO. Han, man. You're van looks pretty good.
HAN. You think so?
GUIDO. Yeah, you've got more talent than I thought. Maybe you should put more of that in your work - maybe you'd get somewhere. *(takes huge hit of a joint, followed by*

his sandwich)
          HAN. Yeah...
          ANNOUNCER. *(off-stage)* Ladies and Gentlemen welcome to the 1974 Barstow County Fair. We will be announcing the winners of the car competitions in 5 minutes. And later, in the center tent, the Battle of Tokyo, and we see who will be crowned the True Shogun of Barstow.
          *(Dr. Vader struts in, with Candy at his side. He's walking proudly, in his Samurai robe over his clothes. He's carrying a padded therapy bat and wearing a black samurai helmet. He's greeting people as though he's the person of honor in a parade, waving imperiously).*
          DR VADER. Hello! Hellooo! Hello good people! I am your savior!
          CANDY VADER. *(crumbling, dropping her face into her palms)* Oh, God.
          PEOPLE IN THE CROUD. Who's that asshole? *(then)* That's the head Republican around here - huge dick. *(then)* Oh. *(then)* It really is, my girlfriend Sandy's cousin, Daisy's seen it. *(then)* Ewww.


                          SCENE 6-A

          STAGE LEFT - WATER PISTOL BOOTH

     *Luke is walking with Princess. They see the water pistol game with big stuffed bears and want to play. Han is trailing behind, but jumps up to challenge Luke at the game. Chewey grabs one of the 6 spots, with Guido and three others. Princess stands by and cheers. The game involves shooting a water-powered pistol into a target -- which looks like a colorful small metal moon with a round dent in it. This drives a spaceship down a track - the first to the end wins. When the ship reaches the end lights go off and possibly a small pyro/sparklers. Luke picks up a pistol and stares down Han, playfully. Han stares back, accepting the challenge.)*

          BARKER. The first one to shoot their ship down the

trench wins the prize! And, 3, 2, 1, go!!

*(Han and Luke both whip up their pistols as though from gun-belts and fire. Luke shoots the water hose – a pneumatic hose with streamer attached – and is winning. Han looking over at the pair, frantic, frustrated.)*

HAN. *(muttering)* Stay on target.
GUIDO. You know Han, you really need to learn to focus, man. Center yourself, you know?

*(Luke is ahead, Han is closing in. Princess is cheering Luke and throws her arm around his shoulder, egging him on. Chewey is playing along, but just enjoying it.)*

PRINCESS. You're doing it. You're doing it! *(The ship reaches the end with a flourish of lights and sounds. Luke wins. Princess jumps up and down, hugs him and kisses his cheek.)*
BARKER. And the prize goes to - this young man and his lovely lady friend!

*(The BARKER hands Princess a giant stuffed animal. Han is furious and storms off. Princess doesn't notice. Han crosses the stage and runs into Priya, alone, holding a box of popcorn. She brightens to see him.)*

PRIYA. Han!
HAN. Hey, Priya. Are you enjoying the fair?
PRYIA. Yes, very much...but you don't look like you're having a good time.
HAN. What? No, it was just a stupid game. I don't even know why I got mad...I don't even want her...that stupid bear.
PRIYA. We all have to find our true path, Hansel. Sometimes it just takes a little while. *(then, offering)* Popcorn?
*(Han takes some, appreciately. They share a moment. Han realizes she likes him - and that he likes her, and has for a long time.)*
HAN. How did you get so smart?
PRIYA. Oh, it helps to have a few lives to figure it out.

*(Han offers his arm to Priya, she acknowledges and takes it, and they walk off together.)*

SCENE 6-B

CENTER STAGE - ILLUMINATES

*The HELMET in the TENT Pavilion is hanging in mid-air from a wire/fishing line about 8-10 feet in the air.. somewhere that you'd need a chair to reach, if you were fairly tall.*

ANNOUNCER. Ladies and Gentlemen, please you're your attention here to the world-famous Shogun Samurai Exhibition brought to you by the Nakamuri Corporation. From the depths of ancient Imperial Japan, comes a genuine replica of the great unifier Toyotomi Hideyoshi's samurai helmet! Given to him by the emperor's Go-Yōzei after the Battle of Nagakute. This event will be a competition worthy of the mighty Shogun as you battle to win the Hideyoshi Helmet.
VADER. YOU WILL BE MINE!
BEN, PRINCESS, CANDY, AIMIEE. *(simultaneously)* Not if I stop you - Don! Dad! Donald! Donny! *(They look at each other, realizing that they're all after Don Vader, and shrug and sharpen their gaze at him thinking 'that makes it easier').*
LUKE. Princess, do you want that helmet?
PRINCESS. Yeah! Oh, really, I just don't want my dad to have it. he's such a pain.
LUKE. Well, then I'll get it for you.
HAN. *(to himself)* We'll see about that.
CHEWEY. *(laughs)*ARRRRR-RRR
GUIDO. That's a cool helmet. Somebody should put that in a movie...
BYSTANDERS. That's got to be worth 50 bucks...Man, that's cool...I bet I could get some chicks with that thing!
BARKER. On the count of three, you will have three minutes to take one of the two chairs and release the helmet from the roof of the pavilion - once you place it firmly on your head, in the style of the old Samurai masters - you are

the winner! You can use your foam bats to stop your opponents from getting to the helmet and putting it on - but please, no fisticuffs!

>BARKER. Three!
>HALF THE CROWD. Two!
>ALL. One!! (WHISTLE SHRIEEEEEKSSSSSSS!!!)
>BARKER. GOOOO!!!!!

*Rumpus music plays, a la "Benny Hill" as a large free-for-all ensues. Individuals pair off and bat each other with the foam bats. Vader is making his way through the crowd. He isn't using the bat - he's using the fist guard to punch people out.*

*Choreography - The floor of the 'pavilion' should be padded with foam mats - (yoga mats, workout mats, something to cushion falls). LUKE and HAN pair off. PRINCESS hitting Han, too. CANDY, AIMIEE and BEN are fighting the by-standers. The movements are quick and natural, as though it were a real foam bat fight.*

*After a minute of individual foam bat fighting, the action focuses on Dr. Vader. The action now slows down into a purposeful slow-motion. Movements are exaggerated and stretched out in breadth and time, as are vocalizations. MUSIC moves from comedic to a WAR DRUM with horns and strings.*

*First, CHEWEY, who is just a little taller than Vader, approaches the chair, rather peacefully, dangling his foam bat and "ARRR-ing." Vader yells "NoooooOoooooo!!!" and knocks him out with a cross, toward the audience. Chewey drops in slow-motion. Vader grabs the chair in slow motion and continues on.*

*Now BEN, AIMIEE and CANDY approach and surround, as Vader gets near the center, underneath the dangling helmet. He is dragging the chair. In three successive blows, he punches Candy, Aimiee and finally Ben with slow-motion jabs and crosses. He jabs Candy, who grabs her chin and falls down, then stomach punches AIMIEE, who doubles over and hits the ground. VADER then brings his arm back, and takes a long cross to Ben's jaw. Ben, facing upstage, stumbles backward as the punch is delivered, falling toward the audience.*

*Finally, LUKE approaches, and Luke and Vader square off. The action returns to standard speed - not slow-motion - They trade glancing blows with the foam bat. Han isn't getting involved, he stands downstage, tensed, with Princess, watching them both.*

*Luke is using his martial arts training to get the better of Dr. Vader, by giving him little blows to the knees and back, as Luke, smaller and faster, moves around him. Finally, having lost all patience, Vader Screams a deafening "ARRRHHHHRHRHRHR!!!" in a slow-motion, stretched out syllables. Princess charges him, Luke charges to protect princess, and Han just stands there, unsure of what he's witnessing. Vader climbs the chair and grabs the helmet. Luke and Princess scream. "NOOOOOO!!!!" as Vader releases it from its hook.*

*A flood of bright light shines on him from behind and above as he grabs the prize straight overhead with outstretched arms. The music swells - strings hold a long high chord - and he lowers it onto his head.*

*The background lights up. The flag of Japan lowers behind Vader, as PRINCESS grasps onto his leg. LUKE strains on the other side, and the rest of the cast is pushing themselves up off the ground, reaching for it, or mortified that Vader has reached it. The tableau freezes at its emotional height, evoking the pattern of the classic 1977 Star Wars poster - it's our 'last supper' image. It's held for 5 seconds ("a button"). The lights go dark.*


## SCENE 6-C

*Lights up on another part of the Fair – minutes later.*

*Dr. V walks through the fair, braggadocio, incredibly proud - he's just punched 1/3 of the people at the fair - everyone's talking about what an asshole he is and glaring - but no one can do anything - he's the Dark Lord! (He's in with the police, RNC coming up and we hear gossip to that effect - 'we can't, he's the committee chairman, and we've got to support the party/Nixon!")*

*Everyone is holding icepacks, folded washcloths, to their eyes, chins, cheeks. Ben is holding an icepack to his jaw. Aimiee is sitting on a chair, holding her stomach. )*

DR VADER. Thanks for being the rungs in my ladder!
BEN *(watching Vader walk by, triumphantly)*. That's it!
AIMIEE. Ben -
BEN. No, I've kept my mouth shut for 16 years, sister. But no more! Donald Vader!
DR. VADER. Oh, Ben... no one wants to hear your drinky drink stories! Drinking! Old Ben. that's our Ben!
BEN. Drink.... my... ass!
BEN. It was 16 years ago.
DR. VADER. No, Ben!
BEN. Korea!
DR. VADER. Ben!
BEN. In a moment of unbridled fear and passion!
DR. VADER. Ben!
BEN. This man took my manly virginity!
DR. VADER. NOOO!
CROWD *(various extras trading lines)*. Well, it's not that surprising... He does seem to be compensating....But he thought he was going to die...Well.. I mean, it was the war.. A lot of weird stuff happens when they're under stress...I've thought of trying that myself!
BEN. Oh...fine. He gives me one in the convection oven and nobody bats an eyelash. Well, here's something for you all. This man screws anything that moves!
CROWD *(murmuring)*. I'd heard that...Yeah, that's true. He really does...That's what he's known for!
BEN. And is the father of at least 8 children in this crowd! You, you, you, you, you - and...*( he winds up and in slow motion, points at Luke)* YOOOOOOOOUUUUUUUU!!!!
AIMIEE. Ben!
DR. VADER. NOOOO!!!
CANDY. AAAHHHH!!!!
PRINCESS. Wha?!

*(Luke is in shock. Aimiee runs to look and holds him. Princess is also in shock, her arms straight and strained, her hands curling up backwards. Vader's head is hung low. Everyone is in a state... except Ben)*

BEN. Oh! Well... I feel better. I feel so much better. *(sees*

*Luke looking angst-ridden).* Well, Lucas, you had to find out sometime. I've been trying to tell you for years, but you're just not the sharpest tool in the shed. But you're a good boy.

AIMIEE. He is a good boy. You are...such a good boy. *(Aimiee hugs him hard, emotionally.)*

DR. VADER *(Vader approaches with some care, deciding on a course of action).* Luke.... I know this is... a shock. I wanted to tell you, but your mother thought it would be best this way. But, no matter... Son, I've been looking out for you - watching you grow.

You're a smart kid. I always... I'll admit something to you, Luke - I've always wanted a son. What I have is a girl who thinks she's a boy, if you know what I mean. Mouth like a sailor! Tough chick. But, a son - someone I can groom to follow in my footsteps... yes... You could be that boy, Luke. You could be that son. If you wanted to be.

LUKE. Well...

DR. VADER. Luke, together you don't know what we could achieve. I'm into some pretty big things, son. Pretty big people. Big men. Powerful. Powerful! It's not just proctology. Luke, join me, and together we could rule the Southern California republican party as father and son! *(Luke sighs, looking anxious.)* But it's not all glamour, son. You'd have to be my apprentice. That means medical school. Proctology is a lucrative field. A lot of anus, Luke. A lot of fistulas. A few carbuncles! Some pretty heinous stuff, I'll be honest. Biblical! But people pay you anything you ask because they're so embarrassed, they just want it to be over. Huh? So, you see, it's got its... rewards. And, like Henry says, You can't reach the stars without looking at a few moons? Huh? Stars? Moon?

LUKE *(breaks free and cries out).* Nooo, noooo noooooooooos! I will never join you.

DR. VADER *(trying a new approach).* Luke! Don't throw your future away. Son, I also practice gynecology. You know what that means, doncha, boy?

*(Luke hangs his head and more or less slinks over to Don, who puts his arm around his shoulder, as they begin to walk away, Don is taking about the glories of his profession, while walking away from crowd with arm around Luke, while the rest look on, dumbfounded.)*

DR. VADER. Why, Luke, you've made the right choice. "Luke Vader, OBGYN, Proctology, and republican .. oh, councilman." How about that? Huh? Yeasss, that puts a smile on your face, doesn't it! Have I ever told you about the time this guy came to me and had a gerbil! Or, was it a vole? I can't remember. Caught in his keister! I have a collection, you know, of 'found objects.' I keep it in a locked cabinet. "Dr. Vader's cabinet of curiosities!"

*(Luke runs away off-stage, dramatically. Don Vader is left alone, realizing that he only has a daughter, who thinks he's a giant ass. He looks back at the crowd who'd been watching him, and tries to play it off.)*

DR. VADER. He'll come around! Crazy kids, huh? Don't know what's good for them! Haha! *(to self)* Wow, this is... embarrassing. *(louder)* He'll come around! Father and son! Ha! Father and son...

SCENE 7

LUKE'S HOUSE - THE NEXT MORNING

*(Luke carries a suitcase across the dusty driveway to his mother's long, finned convertible with a trailer attached. He looks defeated and resigned. Princess, Candy and Don are seeing them off.)*

PRINCESS. *(sheepishly)* Hey, I'm sure you're going to love it.
DR. VADER. Son, let me give you a little fatherly wisdom. *(low, in confidence)* Everything that happens in Vegas, remains in Vegas. *(looks at Princess and Candy)* You know what I mean? *(Dr. Vader pats him on the back jovially, a little too rough. Luke tries to lift the disappointed look from his face, but can't quite.)*
AIMIEE. Ah c'mon. You're gonna make new friends. There are so many opportunities for a young man!

*(Princess looks askance at the implications, even Vader*

*squirms. Vader tears a check out of a checkbook and hands it to Aimiee, who looks at it, smiles and puts it in her bra. Mrs. V watches and looks bothered.)*

    DR. VADER. Now Luke, son. I know it's been a confusing last couple of days, but just about it *(writing in the air)* Vader and Son. "Problems in the rear, we'll be here."
    LUKE. (mortified) Thanks.
    DR. VADER. Okay then. Put 'er there. *(Luke shakes his hand. Dr. Vader steps back and Princess approaches.)*
    PRINCESS. Bye, Luke
    LUKE. Bye, Leah.
    PRINCESS *(brightening, flattered)*. My middle name! I love my middle name. That's my Nana's middle name too... *(softly, close)* I can't believe you remembered!
    LUKE. I remember everything about you.

*(Luke leans in to give her a light kiss on the cheek - she reciprocates. They do it again, but this time, it's lip to lip. They hold the kiss, and soon it's all hands and passion. Aimiee clears her throat. But they keep going at it. Even Vader is getting uncomfortable.)*

    DR. VADER. Okay then! Alright that's affection! That is brotherly-sisterly affection! Yes, Okay then. Okay, break it up! Okay then *(under)* I thought I was the perv.
    AIMIEE. Okay Luke-y, you'll see her again baby. Okay... come on come on, Luke. Luke. Luke...Luke!! Luke! Luke !! Luke!!!

*(Aimiee and Vader step in to pull their kids apart, which requires some effort. The pair emerge dazed, still reaching with their puckered mouths, then locked in each other's eyes. Princess' lipstick is smeared all over both their faces.)*

    PRINCESS. Well, bye. *(She wrinkles her nose flirting. Aimiee herds Luke into the car. He turns and smiles.)*
    LUKE. I love you.
    PRINCESS. I know.

*(Luke gets in the front of the car with his mom, they're ready to go. The back is full of boxes, pots and pans. They're*

*pulling a 4TOW-2U trailer that has green light pouring out of the cracks - it's the pot garden, all packed up. As they're getting in, C3 SKATES UP with a gold suitcase strapped to his back).*

C3. Hey, Mrs. W. I hear you're headed to Vegas? I'm jacked up in this town, got to get my groove on. L-V's the town for me. Going into the casino biz. Razzle dazzle's what I'm talking 'bout. We're doubling down on song and dance. Gonna be big, ya dig.

AIMIEE. Oh, shoot Charlie. We would, but we're packed full.

C3. No worries baby. I don't need a seat, when I got my own wheels. *(pulls out a shiny helmet, inlaid like R2D2's dome, a kind of disco ball with blue and red lights in silver and gold.)*

LUKE. Okay Charlie, grab on!

*(C3 is holding onto a golden water-ski rope coming off of the back of the U-Haul trailer. They start down the road, C3 boogieing with his super dome helmet, with built-in giant headphones. They pass alongside Han and Chewey in the Falcon. Luke smiles, laughs happily. Chewey Arrrrrrs.)*

HAN. Good luck kid. C3!
LUKE. You too!

*(Han nods to Aimiee - does a pistol shot with his finger - see ya! Aimiee winks, points to the back. The trailer is glowing out of the cracks and tin foil around the lid.)*

HAN. See you in Vegas!

*(Continuing along, Han finds the tape under his seat, what's this? It's the sex tape. How did it end up there? Chewey MOANS. Han shrugs and throws it in anger out the window - C3 catches it, and puts it in his tape player.*

*We hear...BOOGIE WONDERLAND*
*We're entering the future --*
*The car pulls away into the golden sun.*

*C3 lets go of the car as it moves offstage and continues*

*his roller-boogie as the LIGHTS CHANGE and the stage transforms from the desert back into the --*

OUTER SPACE DISCO

*Disco ball, fog, and party lights. The entire cast moves onto the empty stage and joins in dancing and getting down to the music. Each cast member in turn separates from the group and dances downstage center, while C3 reads the following:*

AIMIEE became a multi-millionaire madam with a legal sex palace and cannabis nursery on the outskirts of Las Vegas. Every cop within 50 miles knows about it and gets complimentary goods and services.

LUKE stayed in Vegas for 2 years, helping his mother with the nursery. At 19 he ran away to Oregon and opened a karate studio. He still struggles with depression but tries to be cheerful. He's in a long-term monogamous relationship with a nice Jewish girl who looks a lot like his sister.

PRINCESS experimented with her sexuality at Wellesley, moved to New York and invented 'speed dating,' which established her on the NYC scene. She married a baseball player (not a politician) but divorced him because he didn't satisfy her in bed. She remarried and divorced twice more, had a daughter but found she preferred being single. She still thinks of Luke now and again.

CHARLES foresaw Las Vegas becoming an entertainment destination in the 80s and made a daring bet that people would come to see musicals. He helped reinvigorate the Vegas strip and was the first to coin the phrase "Vegas, baby!"

BEN stayed in Barstow and still warms a seat at the Day-Go Bar. He's still looking for Mr. Right.

CANDY left Don in 1981 for her Jamaican aerobics instructor. He took her on a whirlwind romance through the tropics, but left her high and dry after spending her available cash. Don offered to take her back, but Candy thought better of it. She now lives in New York near her daughter and grand-daughter.

DR. VADER ran for State Senate and lost. Disillusioned by politics, Don decided to leave proctology behind and retrained for the new field breast augmentation. He opened a the first speciality clinic in the Central Valley (with a silent partner - Mr. Jabah), and married his 22-year-old secretary, who divorced him and took half. After Nixon resigned, the Dark Lord Kissinger had to remake his empire and chose a new apprentice...*the actor*. There can only be one.

CHEWEY Gruummm Ruurrmmr, rrruuugh and Meerrraaaah, grroormmr, waarrrugh, ahh ahh. But Rrruuumph rummm rummggabbrraa.

HAN stayed in Barstow. He married Priya and look over the Curry Palace when Django retired. Using Han's connections, good work ethic and Priya's common sense and love of the business, they expanded to 5 locations across the Central California Valley. They have 9 kids, and are very happy. Hansel is the true king of Barstow.

GEORGE wrote it all down and went onto create the most successful film franchise in history. And then ruined it.

The MUSIC CONTINUES as C3 leads the full cast disco.

Slowly the stage lights fade out. The cast stand still in the darkness (waiting for the curtain call) and all we see is--

MILLIONS OF STARS

MUSIC FADES. LIGHTS OUT.

### THE END

## ABOUT THE AUTHORS

**Liam Scheff** is the illegitimate son of a wamprat wrangler and an off-duty Imperial cruiser pilot. Or, he is the scion of galactic royalty who abandoned him on a dingy backwater planet to make his hero's journey all the more fulfilling. One or the other.

**S.C.V. Taylor** used to be called Scott, but the Dark Side required that he change his name: it was either S.C.V. or Dooku. He never yells "Yippeee!" though he sometimes thinks it. He is currently working on a way to grill tauntaun healthily.

### Also by Liam:

"Official Stories": is anything we learned in school true, or is it all just an 'official story' designed to protect those in power? *"Official Stories exist to protect officials"* - with this concept as our guide, we peel back the illusion of modernity, dismantling the myths at work in politics and science today. From CIA to JFK and 9/11, HIV and Vaccination to Shakespeare, Darwin, Big Bang and beyond, we'll find out if any of it is true, or if it's all just "official stories."

"The Geneticals": the world's first team of vaccine-damaged superheroes. This lovingly drawn and colored oversided full-color book is exciting, satirical, comedic and instructional, as it plays with one of the most controversial topics of our time. 8x10 full-color.

Summer of '74 Episode 1: Act 1 of "Summer of '74" as a full-color graphic novel.

Official Stories Poster Book: dismantling the "official stories" of our time in words and images. 8.5x11 full-color.

**Also by S.C.V.:**

"Fractured" - The story of a rock and roll siren finding her way in a amid a coterie of ghosts, rock gothica and absinthe. Coming Fall 2013.

## "Summer of '74 - Episode 1" Comic Preview

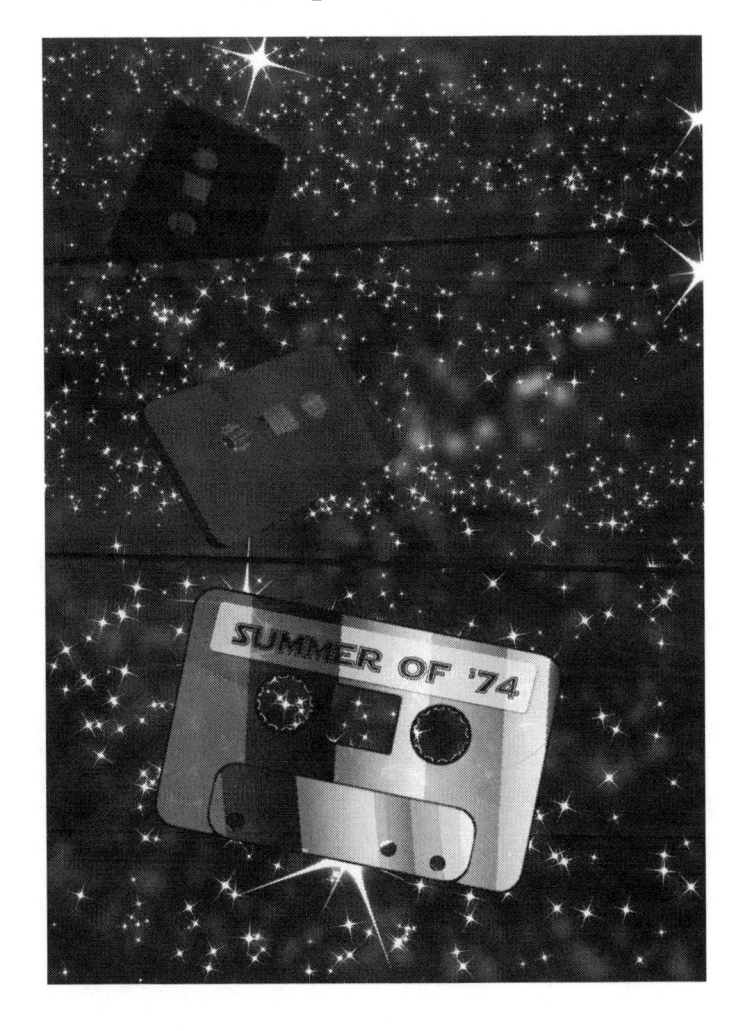

MEANWHILE, DR. VADER IS
TAKING IN THE SCENERY...
WELL, HELLLLLLLLLEEEEEEEEEEEEWWWWWW!
HELLO, MRS. RIGHT!
AND I MEAN,
"RIGHT" NOW!
LET'S SEE WHAT'S
SHAKING DOWNTOWN...
I LOVE THE
SOUTHERN VIEW.
OOOOHHH YEAH.

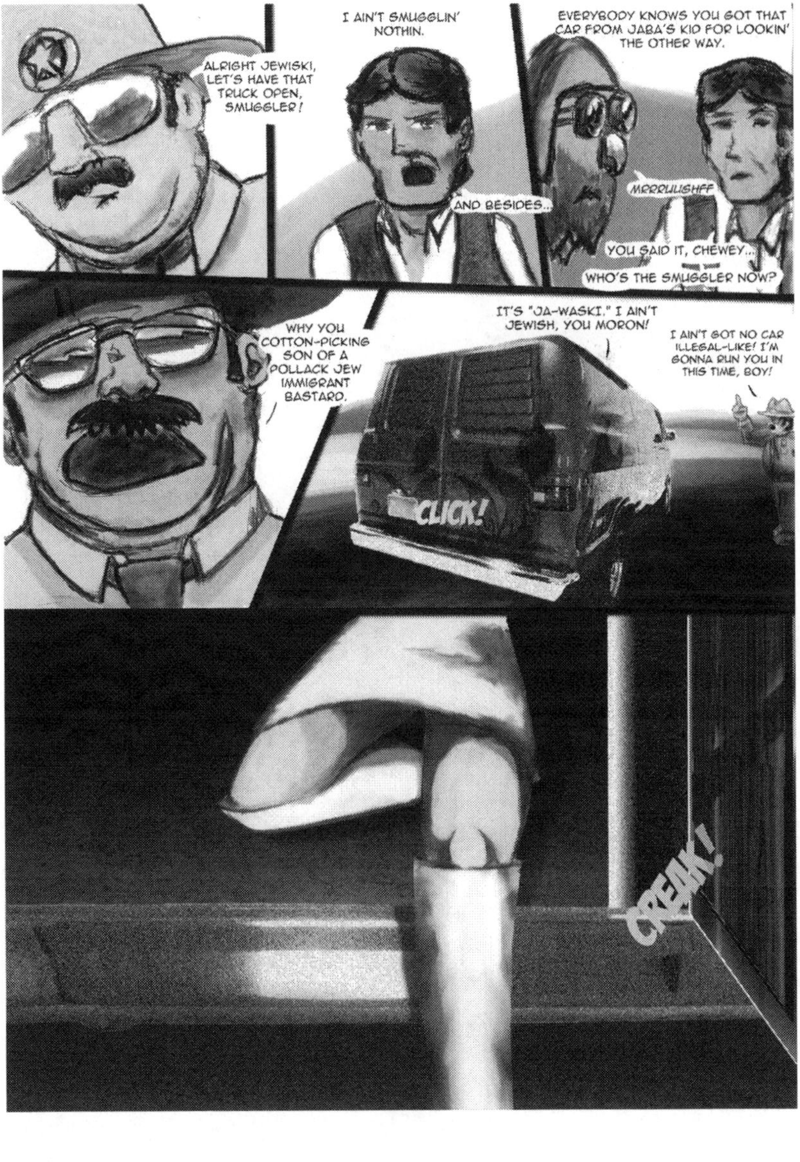
ALRIGHT JEWISKI, LET'S HAVE THAT TRUCK OPEN, SMUGGLER!
I AIN'T SMUGGLIN' NOTHIN.
AND BESIDES...
EVERYBODY KNOWS YOU GOT THAT CAR FROM JABA'S KID FOR LOOKIN' THE OTHER WAY.
MRRRUUSHFF
YOU SAID IT, CHEWEY...
WHO'S THE SMUGGLER NOW?
WHY YOU COTTON-PICKING SON OF A POLLACK JEW IMMIGRANT BASTARD.
IT'S "JA-WASKI." I AIN'T JEWISH, YOU MORON!
I AIN'T GOT NO CAR ILLEGAL-LIKE! I'M GONNA RUN YOU IN THIS TIME, BOY!
CLICK!
CREAK!

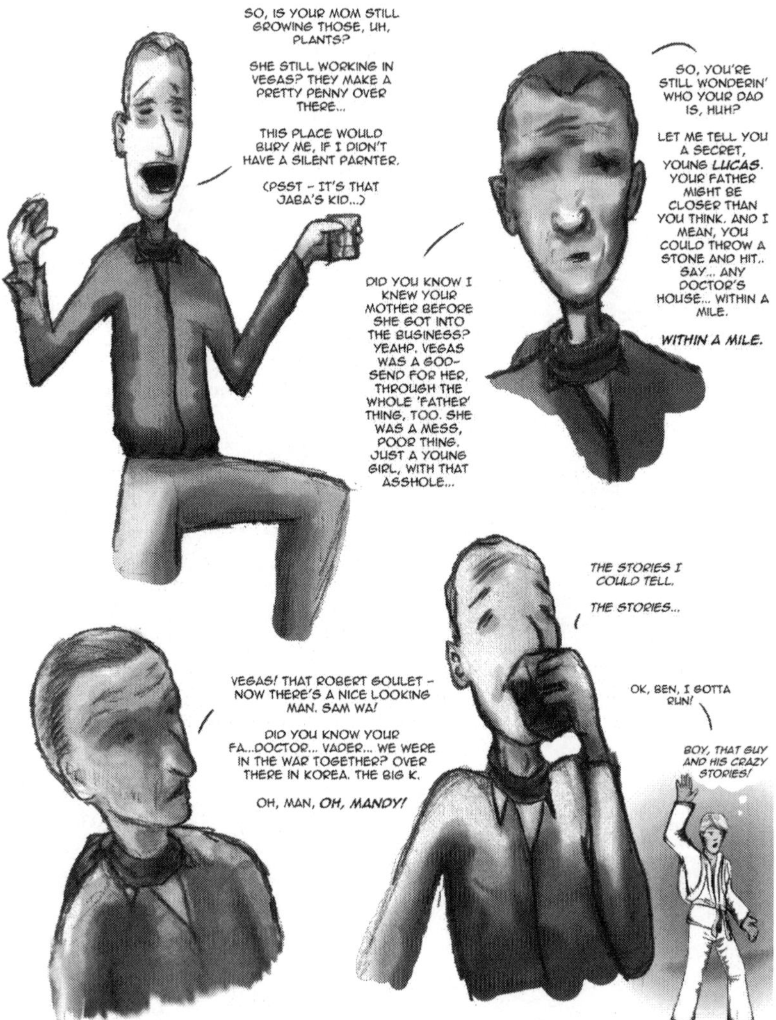
SO, IS YOUR MOM STILL GROWING THOSE, UH, PLANTS?
SHE STILL WORKING IN VEGAS? THEY MAKE A PRETTY PENNY OVER THERE...
THIS PLACE WOULD BURY ME, IF I DIDN'T HAVE A SILENT PARNTER.
(PSST - IT'S THAT JABA'S KID...)
DID YOU KNOW I KNEW YOUR MOTHER BEFORE SHE GOT INTO THE BUSINESS? YEAHP. VEGAS WAS A GOD-SEND FOR HER, THROUGH THE WHOLE 'FATHER' THING, TOO. SHE WAS A MESS, POOR THING. JUST A YOUNG GIRL, WITH THAT ASSHOLE...
SO, YOU'RE STILL WONDERIN' WHO YOUR DAD IS, HUH?
LET ME TELL YOU A SECRET, YOUNG LUCAS. YOUR FATHER MIGHT BE CLOSER THAN YOU THINK. AND I MEAN, YOU COULD THROW A STONE AND HIT.. SAY... ANY DOCTOR'S HOUSE... WITHIN A MILE.
WITHIN A MILE.
VEGAS! THAT ROBERT GOULET - NOW THERE'S A NICE LOOKING MAN. SAM WA!
DID YOU KNOW YOUR FA...DOCTOR... VADER... WE WERE IN THE WAR TOGETHER? OVER THERE IN KOREA. THE BIG K.
OH, MAN, OH, MANDY!
THE STORIES I COULD TELL.
THE STORIES...
OK, BEN, I GOTTA RUN!
BOY, THAT GUY AND HIS CRAZY STORIES!

69

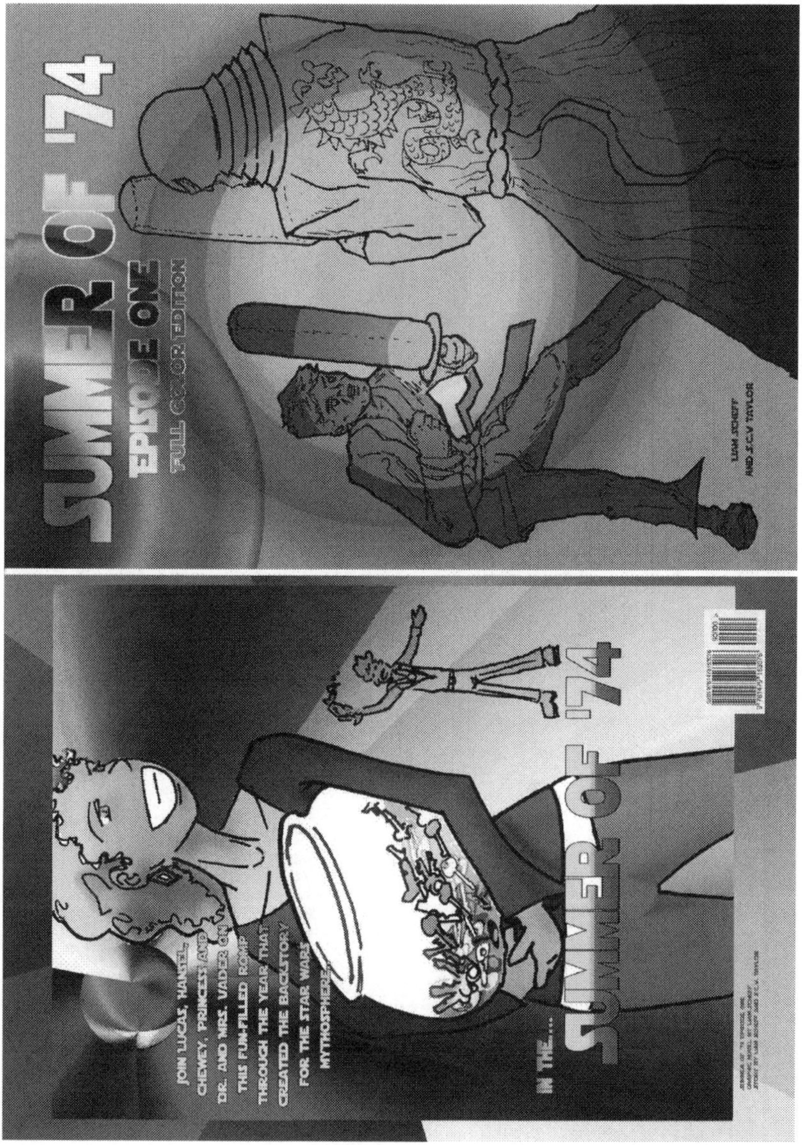
JOIN LUCAS, HANSEL, CHEWEY, PRINCESS AND DR. AND MRS. VADER ON THIS FUN-FILLED ROMP THROUGH THE YEAR THAT CREATED THE BACKSTORY FOR THE STAR WARS MYTHOSPHERE...
IN THE....
SUMMER OF '74
SUMMER OF '74
EPISODE ONE
FULL COLOR EDITION
LIAM SCHEFF
AND S.C.V TAYLOR

THE UNOFFICIAL, UNAUTHORIZED, "TRUE" STORY OF HOW STAR WARS
REALLY BEGAN - IN BARSTOW, CALIFORNIA IN THE...
SUMMER OF '74
WWW.S74COMICS.COM

Made in the USA
Middletown, DE
07 July 2019